Islam: Religion or Fascism?

Islam: Religion or Fascism?

—

William Foltney

ISBN: 1530744059
ISBN 13: 9781530744053
Library of Congress Control Number: 2016905349
CreateSpace Independent Publishing Platform
North Charleston, South Carolina

This book is dedicated to the proliferation of truth

"What is terrible when you seek the truth is that you find it. You find it, and then you are no longer free to follow the biases of your personal circle, or to accept fashionable cliches."

VICTOR SERGE
(QUOTED FROM <u>VILLA AIR-BEL</u>)

"They that observe lying vanities forsake their own mercy."

JONAH

Table of Contents

Islam--Fascism not Religion

——

"WHEN YOU MEET THE UNBELIEVERS, strike the necks" so states the Islam's Koran (47:4). "Strike terror into the hearts of the enemies of Allah" is another directive of the Koran (8:60). This is religion? Or is it bold faced Fascism?

Followers of Fascist causes are driven by a superiority complex that justifies intimidation, propaganda, repression, violence and murder. Fascist violence is based solely on hatred and intolerance of other races, ideologies and/or religions deemed inferior or simply different.

Why is Fascism dangerous? Because it is a political ideology given as a mandate, spread and maintained by force. The ideology is couched in a stated cause. The cause strives for control of entire nations and people groups. Fascist causes dictate how you will salute or bow down as required. The very bounds of your activities of life, what you will do and not do must always conform to the dictates of the leader(s) of the cause. Freedom is not part of the mix.

Islam is one such Fascist political ideology, despite the religious front. Islam exhibits all the destructive behavior patterns of Fascist ideologies seen in history. Hitler's National Socialism (Nazi) was the only political party allowed during his reign in Germany. Likewise, when Islam is in the seat of government power, it is generally the only religion tolerated. Various Islamic factions in rogue nations, vying for supremacy, carry out violence against non-Muslims and other Muslims.

Fascism includes Nazism, Communism, Islam, and any tyrannical political powers. The rights and privileges of individuals under Fascism, including freedom of speech, thought and religion are limited or nonexistent, being subjugated to the will and designs of the totalitarian State.

Militant Islamists are not just a splinter group of Muslims. As of 2010, over 334 million (20%) of the world's Muslims are represented in the 22 Islamic member nations of the Arab League.[1] As Arab League members, Iraq, Egypt, Saudi Arabia, Syria, and the other member countries have agreed to its covenant which calls for the extermination of all Jews and the nation of Israel.

Islamic Fascist intolerance means that hundreds of millions of Muslim children are educated and indoctrinated in the hatred of western nations, Christians and Jews in particular. Just as Nazi Germany's aggression, being Fascist, had to be defeated by armed force in World War Two, militant Islamic geo-politically motivated

---

1 Source: https://en.wikipedia.org/wiki/Islam_by_country and https://en.wikipedia.org/wiki/List_of_Arab_League_countries_by_GDP

aggression in our world today must be met with sufficient force to destroy it from the planet.

Islam is a <u>political cause</u> aimed at world domination through war under the guise of a savage religion. Yet, various sects of Islam and the terrorist groups they spawn can seldom agree on a game plan. This book compares Fascists of the past with militant Islam because Islamic behavior and actions are identical! Mandated religion in the hands of the State is a recipe for trouble. Judge the end product by the results you see.

If Muslims hate Western nations, then why do they migrate there? One reason is the hatred and violence amongst Muslim sects that cannot live and let live. Another reason is, the primary goal of Islam, like other Fascists, is worldwide control.

To survive, America and the free nations of this world must first admit the problem--that Islam is a form of Fascism. It is hoped that exposing Islam for what it is will help America see past the religious face of Islam, and take action to eliminate militant Islam. Further, it will be necessary to educate Muslim populations worldwide to the fact that violent Islam will no longer be tolerated by nations of free men and women.

Fascists say you must live as they tell you. Free people say that you should live your own life and we will live ours.

CHAPTER 1

Fascism means Totalitarianism

———

BARELY ONE WEEK AFTER THE unconditional surrender of Nazi German forces in Europe in World War Two, a detailed report on the war was released by a joint study in the United States Congress, which stated in part:

> *"The Committee feels that out of it all justice will emerge and...a firmer realization that men of all nations and all tongues must resist encroachment of every theory and every ideology that debases mankind."* [2]

What was involved that a Second World War was fought? It was fought to defeat the forces of Fascism, namely the warring powers of Germany, Japan and Italy:

> *"As country after country had fallen to Hitler his carefully reasoned arguments had been split wide open: it was as much the*

---

2 Report of the bi-partisan committee of the Senate and House to the Congress of the United States, May 15, 1945

war of the unemployed laborer as of the Duke of Westminster. Never in the course of history had there been a struggle in which the issues were so clearly defined."[3]

It is only natural that a proper, ordered society should despise evil conduct and impropriety such as murder, rape, theft and threats of violence against a person or family. But there are ideologies on our planet that cannot be tolerated by free peoples because they rest on savage violence and enslavement. In truth, some ideologies in this world are corrupt, even diabolical, and have spread over entire nations, being mandated by the force of governmental laws, terror or both. The result is total control of the populace, such as life under communism, a form of Fascism.

Fascism, under any banner, and freedom cannot coexist. That is because freedom in a society grants or enables people with civil liberties. Civil liberty is defined as "an exemption from the arbitrary will of others, which exemption is secured by established laws, which restrain every man from injuring or controlling another."[4]

One journalist wrote of Fascism as a movement, and expressed his indictment of it because the outcome always brings war:

"training in the history of interlocking ideas and events had provided us with enough intellectual discipline to comprehend the logical imperatives of the movement, to know that

---

3 <u>The Last Enemy</u> by Richard Hillary, 1945, p. 208

4 <u>American Dictionary of the English Language</u> by Noah Webster, First Edition, 1828,

a deliberate assault upon reason made inevitable an assault upon order." [5]

The goal of Fascism is world domination, whether one is talking about German National Socialism (Nazi for short), Italian Fascism, Russian Communism or Islam, a Fascist ideology as this book asserts. Fascists are naturally afraid to allow their own enslaved peoples to experience what life is like in a free country, because that knowledge undermines their control. Communism is one type of Fascism. President Dwight Eisenhower wrote this in regard to the Communism of the Soviet Union in 1952:

> *"It was the adamant insistence of the Communists on maintaining a closed society. Their obdurate attitude was based on fear--fear that once they lifted the Iron Curtain their own people, discovering the goodness and richness of life in freedom, might repudiate Communism itself, and, learning of the sincerely peaceful intentions of free peoples who had been proclaimed to them as deadly enemies, would soon reject the Communist goal of world domination."* [6]

Fascism, a dangerous ideology, has appeared and does appear under various titles throughout a considerable portion of human history. There is often a required mantra, such as a stiff arm salute while declaring "Heil Hitler" in Hitler's Germany, or "there is no God but Allah and Mohammed is his prophet" which recitation is mandatory under Islam. Unfortunately for billions of people, Fascism has been manifested throughout

---

5 <u>Not So Wild a Dream</u> by Eric Sevareid, 1946, p. 94

6 <u>Waging Peace</u> by Dwight D. Eisenhower, 1965, p. 504

much of human history as a religious ideology, in concert with the unyielding force of law. When a religion and the power of government (a nation State) are one and the same, there arises much trouble.

Ironically, the basic characteristics of a religion when it is Fascist in character, is physical brutality, rigid rules and subjugation of the populace by a supreme ruler or rulers with dictatorial power. One must dismiss the thought that peace and goodwill normally follows when government leadership and religion are one and the same.

To the uninitiated, Fascist causes may seem different one from another. But, a closer look offered in this book reveals the stunning similarity of the conduct of Fascists regardless of the era in world history when they existed, or the mask behind which a given Fascist ideology rules and reigns.

The word Fascism has its origin in Italy, under dictator Benito Mussolini, though the concept has been around for a very long time. Nazism was the German version of Fascism. Mussolini came to power in Italy by organizing "fasci," or working men in groups, campaigning for social change. Mussolini's Fascist Party came into being in 1921. Members wore the black uniform of the Arditi, which were the Italian army's storm troopers. "The word 'totalitarianism' was also invented by Mussolini. It decreed (as did the Marxism that Lenin and Stalin inflicted upon Russia) that everyone and every activity came under the direct control of the state. In Italy or Russia, to be apolitical was a punishable offense."[7] Mussolini's brand of

---

7 <u>Blood, Tears and Folly</u> by Len Deighton, 1993, p. 230

Fascism lasted 22 years, ending with the surrender of Italy to the Allied powers, when Allied armed forces began the invasion of Italy.

Make no mistake about Fascist totalitarian leaders. They endanger the planet. One author decreed Mussolini's Fascism and Hitler's Nazism very much akin:

> *"On one point--indispensable to both ideologies--the two men saw eye to eye. Every individual, whatever his station, was a creature of the State, obliged to serve it, even to do violence on its behalf. Intellect was suspect, blind obedience was essential. Gradually Benito Mussolini and Adolf Hitler came to symbolize the State-- all-knowing and all-powerful--in their own persons."[8]*

One form of Fascism that masquerades as a religion today, is Mohammedanism, also known as Islam. Why is Islam Fascism rather than religion? For many reasons, not the least of which is that other major religions on the planet are offered to the hearer on a take it or leave it basis. This is true with Christianity, Hinduism, Sikhism, Buddhism and Shintoism. Islam is not a religion of peace. With Islam, the choice in many countries of the world is to convert to Islam and be ruled by all its laws and its way of life or be killed.

Remember, Fascism is an ideology which debases mankind while demanding total conformance to certain beliefs, philosophies and rules under penalty of death.

"There are a billion-and-a-half Muslims in the world today who worship a prophet who has told them that 'the day of

---

8 <u>Prelude to War</u> by Robert Elson, 1977, p. 82-83

redemption will only come when Muslims fight the Jews and kill them, when the Jews hide behind the rocks and the trees, and the rocks and the trees cry out, Oh Muslim, there is a Jew hiding behind me. Come and kill him.' For a billion and a half Muslims that is the word of God. Denial is one convenient way of dealing with this fact."[9]

Another author compares militant Islam to Hitler's Nazis:

"Backed by state sponsors of terror like Iran, they have become a global threat just as much as the National Socialists were."[10]

Destructive ideologies are ordinarily built on a hodgepodge of wild, even conflicting ideas. These ideologies are expected to be simply obeyed by its subjects, not closely scrutinized:

"Fascism has never really developed a regular literature of its own which tries seriously to interpret the deeper philosophic meaning of that strange creed. Recently, under pressure from Berlin, the Italians have tried to compose a few volumes of that sort and provide the edifice of Fascism with a sound philosophical and historical substructure. The 'apologies' were so evidently written while their authors held their tongues in their cheeks, that no one has been able to take them very seriously..."[11]

---

9 <u>The Black Book of the American Left</u> by D. Horowitz, 2013, p. 393

10 <u>Endgame: The Blueprint for Victory in the War on Terror</u> by Lt. Gen. T. McInerny & Maj. Gen. Paul Vallely, 2004, p. 167

11 <u>Our Battle</u> by Hendrik Willem Van Loon 1939, p. 22-23

Fascist ideologies have come to power over people groups and nations through tyranny, terror, intimidation, extreme violence, open warfare with a geopolitical climate devoid of individual freedom, rights and decision making. While promising a better life, they brook no opposition. There are glaring similarities between Fascist empires such as Adolf Hitler's Germany and today's Islamic dictatorships. One could say that Hitler's National Socialism (Nazism) was a State sponsored religion, because its authoritarian dictates ranged over every facet of life, making it more than a political force, as with Fascist religions of the past and present.

Present day America is not a platform upon which Islam should be examined or judged. This is because unlike the dozens of countries where Islam is the exclusive, State sanctioned religion, the United States of America has freedom of religion and freedom of speech guaranteed by its Constitution. In America, a person can worship as they see fit, or not worship a certain professed deity as he or she pleases. And Muslims in America number only about three million people, or less than one tenth of one percent of the world's 1,670,000,000 Muslims!

The mid-east Arab dictatorships as well as Indonesia and many African republics comprise far and away the lion's share of Islamic peoples. Where Islam is growing the fastest, one can also find a populace that is unarmed, or completely outgunned by armed, violent Muslim terrorists. (Militant Muslims don't take over by popular demand). In Muslim-controlled countries, a person is either a practicing Muslim or his life is in danger. Christianity is not tolerated in countries such as Iran, Pakistan, or Morocco for example. How do those countries and their peoples behave among the family of nations on our planet? Do those countries sanction, train or harbor terrorists? Why do Islamic terrorists cry "death to America?" This book examines those questions by explanations of the purposes and attributes common to Fascist causes.

Islam is a shallow if not hollow (empty) shell of man-made religion, which helps no one and enslaves many. There is always a "cause" stated for the negative behavior characteristic of Fascist ideologies, Islam included. Stated causes which characterize Fascism and the means by which they are empowered, help to identify definite patterns common to all Fascist ideologies of history, as well as present-day threats to peace and freedom in the world.

More about Fascist traits

Fascist ideologies of certain warring nations have been driven home to effected nations under the banner of patriotism, national interests, economic prosperity, or an exclusive, State sponsored philosophy or religion. By studying Fascist ideologies of the past, one can readily identify blatantly Fascist tactics and practices that are glaringly obvious today in militant Islamic nations.

The world today is rife with instances of Islamic terrorism and militarism. Consider and compare the similarity of today's Islamic planned violence with the acts described below of warring Germany in World War Two:

"The trial and punishment of a few assorted Hitlers, Goerings, Ribbentrops, will not end the danger. The conspiracy antedates them; they were only passing agents of it. The record is clear to all who will read it. The master instructors of German

> *militarism long ago began preaching the extension of warfare to whole populations. They advocated mass destruction of people as a part of a philosophy succinctly stated by their military mentor, Von Bernhardi, in his book, <u>Our Future</u>: 'For us there are two alternatives and no third--world dominion or ruin.'"* [12]

Fascism has also been defined as a radical authoritarian nationalism. It attempts to unify a nation or people group through veneration of the State, devotion to a strong leader, and emphasis on ultra-nationalism and militarism. Make no mistake about it, a religion can be Fascist in nature, if the religion has the power of the government behind it or it is openly and exclusively State-sponsored. This is because government, with the force of law, dictates the very actions and thoughts of its citizenry.

State sponsored and sanctioned religion, with its exclusivity, has brought out the worst in mankind in prominent religions such as the Roman Catholic Church as well as the Church of England. Both exhibited strong Fascist tendencies in their past behavior because they persecuted, tortured and murdered dissenters. An example of each of those two religion's Fascist behavior is given below.

ROMAN CATHOLICISM IS NOT BIBLICAL CHRISTIANITY

Worse yet, the Roman Catholic Church was Fascist in its conduct during the so-called dark ages, and faces the wrath of Islam for its former warring against Muslims.

---

12 <u>This Must Not Happen Again! The Black Book of Fascist Horror</u> by Clark Kinnaird, 1945, p. 8

BACKGROUND OF THE CHRISTIAN FAITH: INDIVIDUAL CHOICE

James Madison along with Thomas Jefferson took the lead in moving the Commonwealth of Virginia toward the <u>disestablishment</u> of the Episcopal Church in 1774, by denying public funds to the clergy. Popular sentiment, aroused by liberals and religious dissenters convinced the Virginia Assembly to enact the thorough Bill for Religious Liberty. Madison had written and circulated a classic defense of the principle of religious freedom which pointed to the sharp separation of church and state that Madison would later write into the Bill of Rights of the United States Constitution.

Fundamental to the understanding of what was at stake here, Madison wrote and circulated in great detail an explanation of the necessity for freedom of religion prior to the passage of the Virginia Bill for Religious Liberty. An excerpt reads:

> *"Because we hold it for a fundamental and undeniable truth, religion or the duty which we owe to our Creator and the manner of discharging it, can be directed only by reason and conviction, not by force or violence. The religion of every man must be left to the conviction and conscience of every man; and it is the right of every man to exercise it as these may dictate. This right is in its nature an unalienable right."* [13]

It is axiomatic that freedom and Fascism cannot co-exist. Through the centuries, when a religion becomes the officially sanctioned, sole religion of a State or nation, trouble follows because religious

---

13 <u>The Mind of the Founder, Sources of the Political Thought of James Madison,</u> 1973, p. 7

freedom, freedom of thought, freedom of speech and liberty of conscience are criminalized.

The Christian religion is based on the premise that its god, the LORD, God of all creation, brought forth His only Son, whose name is Jesus Christ, in the womb of a virgin. Jesus was born without a human father (God was His Father), who lived a sinless life, and then voluntarily allowed Himself to be killed in a cruel, substitutionary death for sinful humans. Thus, Christianity teaches that a human being can be reconciled to God through God's own sacrifice. The Holy Bible tells mankind that accepting God's Son, Jesus Christ, as his Savior means the payment for one's sins committed is paid. Such a person becomes justified with God and fit for Heaven when this life ends:

> *"God, who at sundry times and in divers manners spake in time past unto the fathers by the prophets, Hath in these last days spoken unto us by his Son, whom he hath appointed heir of all things, by whom also he made the worlds; Who being the brightness of his glory, and the express image of his person, and upholding all things by the word of his power, when he had by himself purged our sins, sat down on the right hand of the Majesty on high;"* [14]

While looking to the twelve close disciples of Jesus Christ in the church at Jerusalem, all local assemblies of Christian churches were congregational, meaning each was independent of any earthly authority. This Bible principle means that the Christian church had no earthly headquarters. The church is headed by Jesus Christ, now in Heaven and whose imminent return to earth to receive all

---

14 <u>Authorized (King James) Bible</u>, 1789, Book of Hebrews 1: 1-3

those into Heaven who have trusted Christ, whether living or dead at His coming. His return is at an unknown day and time in the future, which all Christians await.

The Holy Bible message of belief in God is expressly offered through one mediator only, Jesus Christ, the incarnate Son of God. It is hastened to point out that that Bible message is offered peacefully, without coercion. Quoting Jesus Christ himself:

> *"Come unto me, all ye that labour and are heavy laden, and I will give you rest. Take my yoke upon you, and learn of me; for I am meek and lowly in heart: and ye shall find rest unto your souls. For my yoke is easy, and my burden is light."* [15]

And what exactly is the end result or fulfillment of accepting the tenets that the Christian Holy Bible puts forth? Again, word for word, as spoken by Jesus Christ:

> *"My sheep hear my voice, and I know them, and they follow me: And I give unto them eternal life; and they shall never perish, neither shall any man pluck them out of my hand. My Father, which gave them me, is greater than all; and no man is able to pluck them out of my Father's hand."* [16]

While there were wars directed against the enemies of the nation of Israel in the Old Testament of the Bible, this was primarily before Israel was restored to their homeland which the LORD gave them. This was after four hundred years in bondage in Egypt, about 1450

---

15 <u>Authorized (King James) Bible</u>, 1789, Book of Matthew 11: 28-30
16 Ibid., John 10: 27-29

B.C. Many other nations and people groups were driven out of the land of Israel because of idolatry including sacrificing children to idols. The Jewish religion today continues in the form and formality of early Jewish worship as given by Moses and the prophets of the Old Testament.

But in the gentile world (non-Jewish), the New Testament portion of the Holy Bible reveals the story of the fulness of God's plan of redemption. This is through someone who is more than a prophet, it is God's own Son, Jesus Christ. The Christian church was started by Jesus Christ himself. Followers of Jesus Christ were first called Christians in Antioch, Syria about 41 A.D.[17]

The New Testament unfolds the message of a merciful and gracious God who offers the peaceful message of eternal life (quoted above), as well as the prophecy of the future destruction of planet Earth, and to that point in the future where time itself ends and eternity begins. The offer of new life in Jesus Christ and eternal life through Him is on a free will basis. In other words, each person can decide for themselves whether to believe what the Holy Bible states.

Violence against ones enemies is not at all in the picture in the Christian faith, as divulged in the New Testament of the Holy Bible. In fact, quite the opposite is taught repeatedly, such as these words spoken by Jesus Christ:

"Ye have heard that it hath been said, Thou shalt love thy neighbour, and hate thine enemy. But I say unto you, Love your

---

17 <u>Authorized (King James) Bible</u>, 1789, Book of Acts 11:26

enemies, bless them that curse you, do good to them that hate you, and pray for them which despitefully use you, and persecute you;" [18]

There is free will in the Christian faith. Unlike Islam, with its very strict rules about certain days of the year, Christians are admonished to worship the LORD God, but not to worry whether someone else lives and worships exactly on the schedule or timetable that they do:

" *One man esteemeth one day above another: another esteemeth every day alike. Let every man be fully persuaded in his own mind."* [19]

The known world heralds the birth of Jesus Christ annually, which is celebrated in the event known as Christmas each December. There is no violence connected with this special holiday. Nor is violence in the picture surrounding Jesus Christ's life of thirty-three years on the earth, nor his death, burial and resurrection from the grave. We would note that Jesus Christ's resurrecting bodily (return to life from the grave) after being dead for three days was seen in person by many people over a period of forty days, in one instance by upwards of five hundred men. [20]

---

18 Ibid., Matthew 5:43-44
19 Ibid., Romans 14:5
20 <u>Authorized (King James) Bible</u>, 1789, Book of First Corinthians, chapter 15, v. 6

ROME ENFRANCHISED CATHOLIC RELIGION FOR THE WHOLE WORLD: OBEY OR DIE

The peaceful nature of the Christian religion, however, was entirely altered several hundred years after death of Jesus Christ. A group of local church elders or pastors assembled who were misguided or simply men without Christ. These men conceived the idea that an earthly hierarchy should be contrived exercising authority over all local Christian churches. This despite the fact that the Holy Bible names no earthly headquarters for the Christian faith whatsoever.

This is one principal reason why what became known as the Roman Catholic Church is <u>not</u> part of the Christian faith, because of its claims to not only be a part of the Christian faith, but that it is the earthly head of Christianity worldwide. Its heretical and unscriptural teachings and practices reveal its character as a form of religion, but not the Christian faith or religion.

Many un-biblical doctrines surround Catholicism, not the least of which is the claim that Simon Peter, a disciple of Jesus Christ, was the first "Pope" (Father) or earthly head of the church. This is put forth despite the fact that James, the half brother of Jesus was clearly in charge of the church at Jerusalem, not Peter. Nor is there any record in the Bible that Peter was ever in Rome, as the Roman Catholic church claims. Also, Peter was married, according to the Bible. Yet the Catholics claim celibacy for all priests and high officials including the "Pope."

The Roman Catholic Church was organized about 321 A.D., claiming Divine authority and power to rule over local Christian churches. Again, this is without any basis in the Holy Bible, the sole authority for the Christian faith. This power was created in the name of religion but without Biblical authority, and it went straight to their heads. Religious power in the hands of the wrong people, usually spells trouble. In its megalomania, the Roman Catholic church hierarchy carried out systematic violence in the name of religion for many centuries, while it could get away with it, with its claims of authority over all churches. Remember, there is no such directive to carry out violence on behalf of the Christian faith! It is a matter of free will for each person.

A reign of government-sanctioned Roman Catholic terror was commissioned and empowered by the head of this monster religion, whose title was Pope or Pontiff. This followed the adoption of the Roman religion by Roman Emperor Constantine as the official State religion of the government of Rome, which ruled the known world at the time of Constantine, with kings and kingdoms answerable to the Roman Pontiff for centuries. The Emperor Constantine supposedly saw a vision of a great cross and declared himself a Christian, and then mandated that everyone under His domain declare themselves to be a Christian under the authority of the Roman Pontiff.

Throughout a period of over 1,000 years called the Dark Ages, more than 50 million people were murdered by drowning, burning at the stake, or other cruel forms of execution when the Roman Catholic church and the State became synonymous under Rome.[21] The victims were those who would not confess the Pope

---

21 <u>The Trail of Blood</u> by J. M. Carroll, 1928, p. 36-38

as the vicar (meaning one who is standing in the place of) of Jesus Christ. It also included those who would not conform to Roman Catholic doctrines including the baptism of infants and the doctrine of Maryolatry (veneration of Mary, the mother of the incarnate Christ, worshipped by Catholics as the mother of God and part of the godhead). God has no mother.

Military campaigns sanctioned by the Roman Catholic Church in the Middle Ages also affected other religions. Violent attacks by the Roman Catholic Church under auspices from Roman rulers were aimed at the Middle East, and were called "The Crusades." They were first ordered by Pope Urban II in 1095 A.D., the idea being to restore access to Jerusalem, which Rome once ruled. Israel is called the Holy Land in reference to the historic home of Jews and where Jesus Christ was killed. These military conquests went on for 200 years.[22]

Literally hundreds of thousands of Roman Catholics from different countries of Western Europe enlisted as crusaders for the Pope. Pope Urban II promised those who went to war that they would be forgiven of their sins, an ill-bred promise at best.

In addition to demonstrating devotion to the Roman Catholic Church, The Crusades provided opportunities for economic and political gain for the Roman Empire. The People's Crusade prompted the murder of thousands of Jews and Muslims, and is a source of ill will toward Christians by Muslims today, as Muslims assume the Roman Catholic religion is part of Christianity, which it is not.

---

22 https://en.wikipedia.org/wiki/Crusades

One example of Roman Catholic State sponsored violence, is that of Michael Sattler. Sattler, a professing Christian, had his tongue cut out, and hunks of flesh cut from his body before being burned alive on May 25, 1527 by the Pope-appointed authority of King Ferdinand of Austria. His offense was proclaiming the promise of Heaven to all who would trust Jesus Christ of Nazareth as personal Savior by faith in Christ's substitutionary death, burial and resurrection from the dead. Sattler also declared infant baptism as an unbiblical fabrication of Roman Catholicism.

Sattler's wife and twelve others were also arrested and murdered. She was killed by cruel drowning, when likewise they all refused to recant faith in Jesus Christ alone for the salvation of the soul, and would not confess the Roman Catholic Pope as God's supreme authority on the earth. [23]

The Roman Catholic Church has an un-Biblical organizational hierarchy of priests, bishops, archbishops, and cardinals on up to its head, a so-called Pontiff or Pope, which means father or papa. Catholic doctrine forbids their religious clerics, called priests, to marry.

There are no priests in the New Testament of the Holy Bible, except believers in Jesus Christ who are referred to as a holy priesthood (I Peter 2:5). Church leaders are instead called bishops, elders, pastors, and deacons. The irony about celibacy for Catholic priests is that priests in the Jewish religion detailed in the Old Testament of the Bible were in fact married. Roman Catholic celibacy for

---

23 The Anabaptist Story by William Estep, 1963, p. 43-44

priests has compounded that religion's financial problems, with jury awards from lawsuits against Roman Catholic diocese across the United States, for Catholic priests sodomizing literally thousands of young boys.

The 2004 John Jay Report for the U.S. Conference of Catholic Bishops was based on a study of 10,667 convictions against 4,392 priests for engaging in sexual abuse of minors between 1950 and 2002. As of 2009, U.S. Catholic Dioceses have paid out $2,600,000,000 (that's billion not million) in sexual abuse cases, most for sexually abusing young boys. This has resulted in many U.S. Catholic dioceses filing bankruptcy protection (such as the Minneapolis Diocese in 2015), and have resulted in thousands of Catholic schools and "parishes" closed and sold to pay damage awards.

The Catholic religious system calls itself the "Most Holy Roman Catholic Church." There is nothing holy about the molesting and sodomizing of young boys by sodomite priests. Millions of Catholics follow this man-made religion full of ritual and formality, having been told over and over that the Catholic church is the true church, which it is not, seemingly oblivious to the widespread immorality of its "clergy."

Human beings are innately religious, but the fruits of any religion reveal its true character. Millions of people are members of this Roman Catholic religion today, because they are so totally without knowledge and understanding of the Holy Bible. But Roman Catholicism is a benign power in our day.

THE CHURCH OF ENGLAND

Remember, "State religion" generally means the abolition or pro-hibition of the existence or practices of any other religion, thus dictating the form, formality and practices of the official State re-ligion in every day life. Thus it was in like fashion, the Church of England persecuted religious believers who would not follow its beliefs, or who spoke against its teachings. The English Crown stood behind the Church of England, which came into being by declaration of England's immoral King Henry VIII.

The king announced that the Church of England was now separate from Rome, after the Roman Catholic Pope refused to grant the king a divorce from his wife. But as with Rome, de-viation from the authority, the hierarchy and the doctrines of the Church of England was subsequently not tolerated for a period of several centuries. Fascist violence and control of an entire nation was conducted by the Crown of England in the name of religion. To the untrained observer this would naturally constitute behavior exactly the opposite of what any religion is supposed to represent!

Joan Boucher, known as Lady Joan of Kent in England, was a lady of note, possessing much wealth. She was well known at the palace in the days of King Henry VIII and King Edward VI. But as an Anabaptist Christian, she devoted her life to the study of Tyndale's English translation of the Holy Bible. She was arrested for sharing her faith in Jesus Christ. Then for two weeks, two bishops of the Church of England kept her and attempted to dissuade her of her faith. But she would not confess the supreme authority of the Church of England, and rejected the extra-Biblical doctrine of the immaculate conception of Mary, the mother of the incarnate Christ.

She also would not recant her faith. So, she was subsequently tortured then burned at the stake on May 2, 1550. Being preached to by Bishop Scorey as the flames rose around her, she declared to him and all who heard, "You lie like a rogue. Go read the Scriptures."[24]

Another typical example of brutal, Fascist behavior of the Church of England was the case of the Reverend John James. As he was preaching from the Bible on October 19, 1661, in his church at Whitechapel, London, a justice of the peace entered to disperse the assembly. He ordered Mr. James to cease preaching, which the little man promptly declined to do. The official had him taken from the pulpit by force and conveyed to Newgate Prison.

Reverend James was charged with having used seditious language in his sermon. He appeared in court, pleading not guilty, but was remanded to prison after a guilty verdict was given against him upon the evidence of profligate witnesses. Mrs. James subsequently petitioned King Charles II to intercede for her husband, but the king treated her with contempt and decreed that the sentence of death by hanging must be fulfilled.

His last words were for the King, "The Lord Jesus Christ, the Son of God, is the King of England." Immediately after execution, his body, separated into parts, was affixed to the gates of the city, and his head set upon a pole by the meeting place where, along with his people, he had worshipped God in peace.[25] This sounds a great deal like today's Islamic violence, does it not?

---

24 The History of the Baptists, by Thomas Armitage, 1976, p. 449-450
25 This Day in Baptist History by E. Wayne Thompson & David Cummins, 1993, p. 433-434

State Religion in colonial America

America has seen Fascist behavior in regard to religion, in its infancy. In the 1700's, Virginia, Massachusetts and several other colonies, laws were passed enabling an established state church supported by public taxes, mandating church attendance, and forbidding the worshipping of any other religious sects. Some type of state church existed in all five southern American colonies, as well is in Connecticut and New Hampshire.[26]

> *"In South Carolina as early as 1706, the Board of Trade approved a new law establishing the Church of England with support from public funds. In North Carolina in 1732, a law was passed establishing the Church of England."*[27]

Efforts to legislate religion in Virginia continued for decades. The following law was enacted on December 14, 1662:

> *"Whereas many schismatical persons out of their averseness to the orthodox established religion, or out of new fangled conceits of their own heretical inventions, refused to have their children baptized. Be it therefore enacted by the authority aforesaid, that all persons that, in contempt of the divine sacrament of baptism, shall refuse when they carry their child to lawful minister in that country to have them baptized shall be amersed two thousand pounds of tobacco, half to the publique."*[28]

---

26 <u>Colonial America</u> by O.T. Bark, Jr. & Hugh Lefler, 1968, p. 391
27 <u>This Day in Baptist History</u> by E. Wayne Thompson & David Cummins, 1993, p. 15
28 Ibid., p. 522

Monetary fines, public beatings and imprisonment were punishments used for violating state church laws, but were eventually overcome by the spread of biblical, Christian faith. Freedom of religion in America was guaranteed by the very first amendment to the Constitution of the United States, which became effective December 15, 1791.[29] This law was a direct result of Baptist and other Separatist preachers who were willing to be incarcerated, beaten and fined in order to attain liberty of conscience in religious practices.

One must remember that Fascism sets the world on fire because of its inherent paranoid and megalomaniac character. The four corners of the world suffered under Nazi Germany's Fascism in World War Two. Today, Islam intends to inflame the world once again in the blood of countless innocents because of the inherent hatred and intolerance of all those who will not adhere to Islam's savage, arbitrary, and immoral tenets. Islamic-ruled countries such as Saudi Arabia, one of the richest per capita nations on the planet, have the resources to offer help in stopping Islamic terrorism. Instead, they spawn terrorism, which lends credibility to the statement that Muslims are not opposed to murder in the name of their "religion."

Saudi Arabia, as Sunni Muslims, definitely supports Islamic terrorism. Nineteen of the twenty-one airline hijackers of the terrorist attacks in America on September 11, 2001 were in fact Saudi Arabian citizens.

---

29 The Constitution of the United States Independence Hall, Philadelphia, 1787

Russian Communism is Fascism

This treatise primarily centers on comparisons of the ideologies of Nazi Fascism and Islamic Fascism because there are such striking and unmistakable resemblances of the two in attitudes, propaganda, and violent conduct. Yet we recognize that there are other examples of Fascism in history and in the present day. "Hitler and Stalin had much in common as totalitarians, and their systems of government were akin."[30]

The Union of Soviet Socialist Republics (USSR) is a Fascist, totalitarian State and may have disintegrated for a time, but now that western capital has come in to breakaway republics bordering Russia, the USSR is taking action to retake its former empire and territories while daring any other nation or international power to oppose them:

> *"Putin is a corporatist (the economic doctrine of Fascism). He's a dictatorial, charismatic leader who bends church, business, labor and media to the needs of a centralized state under a thoroughly nationalist banner."*[31]

Fascist ideology views political violence, war and imperialism as a means to achieve rejuvenation, and asserts that stronger nations also have a right to expand their territory by displacing weaker nations. Fascism consistently invokes the primacy of the State by the authoritarian actions of the rulers. Opposing any plans or decisions of Stalin's communist regime was a capital crime as such persons were

30 <u>Their Finest Hour</u> by Winston Churchill, 1949, p. 133
31 <u>The Well-Worn Fascist Lies of Putin</u> by Jonah Goldberg, Tribune Media, May 28, 2014

deemed an enemy of the State, a saboteur or a counter-revolutionary.[32] Consider the mass murders committed by Joseph Stalin in Russia:

> *"The Great Purge in which Tukhachevsky died began in the same summer as my visit to Russia and was already in progress while I was inside the USSR. News of it filtered through in isolated reports of proceedings against various government officials, then with a tremendous shock to Western Europe, the news burst upon the world in June 1937 that Marshal Tukhachevsky, the popular hero of the Russian people, the architect of the Red Army, had been executed. The purge extended until--according to reports--Stalin had liquidated 75 percent of the members of the Supreme War Council, eliminating, besides three marshals and thirteen generals, an estimated 1,500 high-ranking officers, while thousands of others disappeared into prisons and labor camps.*
>
> *But this was only among the military command; the purge swept through every branch of the Soviet Government and people; estimates of the number of victims ranged from 8 to 20 million of the USSR's 200 million population. The number included Trotskyites, Mensheviks, anarchists, Jews, priests, intellectuals, civil servants, eventually workers and peasants, and even foreign Communist leaders, such as the Hungarian Bela Kun and the German Max Hoelz, who disappeared without a trace."* [33]

What kind of society is created and sustained under Fascism? A secret, oppressive society! Under Joseph Stalin, Russia confiscated

32 <u>The Harvest of Sorrow</u> by Robert Conquest, 1986, p. 186
33 <u>Master of Spies</u> by General Frantisek Moravec, 1975, p. 90-91

all privately owned farms. They were taken over permanently without compensation by the central government in favor of government-run collective farms. The results have showed, over many decades, a severe reduction in agricultural output as the populace lost the incentive to work, seeing as one's own hard work no longer counted for any reward appropriate with one's own diligence or extra effort:

> *"The socialist economy could not even create sufficient growth to feed its own people. Once the breadbasket of Europe, Soviet Russia became under socialist planning a chronic importer of grain, an economy of forced rationing and periodic famine."*[34]

The starvation of millions of Ukrainians in the early 1930's under Russian communism is well known, as their entire crops, small as they were, were taken away by Stalin's central government:

> *"In the course of our official tours I saw slave labor for the first time in my life. Prisoners working on the Volga-Moscow canal and the construction site of the new House of the Red Army, now a Moscow showplace, were under the supervision of armed uniformed guards. Most of these workers were women dressed in rags and sacking. Ninety percent of these unfortunates, I learned, were wives of Kulaks, farmers who had resisted collectivization of the their land and had been sent to the Siberian mines.*

---

34 <u>The Black Book of the American Left</u> by D. Horowitz, 2013, p. 267

> *The fate of these peasants, I thought, typified the at-*
> *titude toward human life which I had already noticed in*
> *dealing with our new allies. The famine and terror which*
> *had accompanied the Soviet agriculture reforms had been*
> *carefully concealed from the outside world. But there had*
> *been reports of millions perishing as the starving peasants*
> *reverted to cannibalism, fought for their land with pitch-*
> *forks against army units and were butchered or deported*
> *en masse."[35]*

Such reports as this, of the forced starvation of five million Ukranian peasant farmers in the 1930's, are common. Communism is simply left-wing Fascism, plain and simple.[36] A former left-wing American radical had this to say about the Fascism under Stalin:

> *"In the society we hailed as a new human dawn, tens of mil-*
> *lions of people were confined in slave-labor camps, in con-*
> *ditions rivaling Auschwitz and Buchenwald. Between 30*
> *and 40 million people were killed, in peacetime, in the daily*
> *routine of socialist rule. While leftists applauded the Soviet*
> *Union's progressive policies and guarded its frontiers, Soviet*
> *Marxists killed more peasants, more workers, and even more*
> *Communists than all the capitalist governments together since*
> *the beginning of time...it was only the CIA that actually made*
> *the crimes public.."[37]*

---

35 <u>Master of Spies</u> by General Frantisek Moravec, 1975, p. 54-55
36 <u>The Black Book of the American Left</u> by D. Horowitz, 2013, p. 160
37 Ibid., p. 178

Joseph Stalin, dictator of Fascist Russia, was no different during wartime with his own military forces. His iron grip was felt through the Communist party hierarchy and communicated to the military:

> *"The slightest divergence from its wishes, or indeed failure or bad luck, meant being worked to death in a slave labor camp or summary execution. When Stalin added 'or you will answer with your head' to his commands it was not a joke. By the time the war ended 238 generals and admirals had been executed, or had died in penal battalions, simply because they had failed to win."* [38]

Where does Fascism come from? In the opinion of Winston Churchill:

> *"Fascism was the shadow or ugly child of Communism. While Corporal Hitler was making himself useful to the German officer class in Munich by arousing soldiers and workers to fierce hatred of Jews and Communists, on whom he laid the blame of Germany's defeat, another adventurer, Benito Mussolini, provided Italy with a new theme of government which, while it claimed to save the Italian people from Communism, raised himself to dictatorial power. As Fascism sprang from Communism, so Nazism developed from Fascism."* [39]

While Fascism--violent, authoritarian dictatorship--today is present in the world under the name of "Islam", one must remember

---

38 <u>Blood, Tears and Folly</u> by Len Deighton, 1993, p. 453
39 <u>The Gathering Storm</u> by Winston Churchill, 1948, p. 15

that Fascism has appeared in other places as a sort of "religious philosophy" earlier, for example, under Russian communism as developed by Lenin and Stalin. Totalitarian dictatorship in the name of a cause which cannot be altered or opposed, is the name of the game, whether communism or a religion such as Islam that demands total obedience.

America's first Secretary of Defense, James Forrestal warned officials in the Truman Administration that Russian ideology was dangerous, and that it was lurking in the form of foreign agents in countries around the world. Forrestal spoke of Russian Fascism as follows:

> *"Nothing about Russia can be understood without understanding the implacable and unchanging direction of Lenin's religion-philosophy"* [40]

Communism, like Fascism, exists like a kind of exclusive religion. Yet, ironically, religion is opposed. As Lenin stated in a letter in 1913, of the Communist Party's position:

> *"Every religious idea, every idea of God, even flirting with the idea of God, is unutterable vileness..."* [41]

The Soviet Union (Russia) was allied with Great Britain and the United States in the Second World War in the monumental task of ridding the world of the common enemy of Nazi Fascism. However, the Soviets proved in many ways, before the war ended,

---

40 The Candy Bombers by Andrei Cherny, 2008, p. 164
41 The Harvest of Sorrow by Robert Conquest, 1986, p. 199

that though we were allied with them in a common cause, Russia was also the enemy of any and all free nations!

For example, U.S. Army Air Force B-29 Superfortress bombers on occasion were either short of fuel or damaged by Japanese flak or fighter shells, and had to land at Russian air fields when returning from bombing raids on Japan. In at least four instances, the ten-man B-29 crews were confined by Russian military forces and grudgingly released back to U.S. forces, while the Russians kept our giant bombers, which were never returned. The U.S. State Department, in its usual weakling fashion, registered a protest with the Russian embassy and President Truman also cowered, and did nothing more about the matter. These Russians are our allies? The Russians replicated the B-29 bomber in their own clumsy version of a heavy bomber shortly after the end of World War Two.[42]

Dictator Stalin also mocked America and all it stood for by his conduct throughout the Second World War, even as we came to Russia's aid in their war effort. The U.S. delivered 400,000 jeeps and heavy trucks, 12,000 tanks and other armored vehicles, 11,400 airplanes, 4.4 million tons of food, 1,900 steam railroad locomotives and over 10,000 railroad cars to Russia to fight the Nazi invasion of Russia. All of these war goods were not politely requested, they were rudely demanded by Soviet Premier Joseph Stalin, the mass murderer of millions of his own people. Fascists dictate. Our American governmental leaders put up with Stalin's tirades and complaints along the way, only because we were fighting a common enemy.

---

42 <u>Point of No Return </u>by Wilbur Morrison, 1979, pp. 133-134

Less than three years after the World War Two armistice, the Soviet Union tried to provoke the United States to war with their blockade of west Berlin. (See Chapter 15 of this book for that saga.)

Just five years after America had spent $11 billion[43] supplying the Soviet Union with armaments, vehicles, aircraft, food and supplies to help Russia survive the Nazi onslaught (as just enumerated), the Soviets led their new Communist/Fascist protectorate nation of North Korea on the warpath. North Korea attacked its neighbor to the south, to take yet more territory by force. The effort was called the Korean War (more on this in Chapter Two of this book, under the sub-heading 'Fascism of today.')

The common thread with Fascism is loss of freedom with supremacy of a central government. The Kremlin announced on June 23, 1941, "Once and for all the Finns are to be exterminated from the surface of the earth."[44] At that time, Finland President Rysto Ryti gave a very accurate description of what Communism and Fascism really are, as his nation of 4 million people battled in war against the attacking Soviet Union with its 130 million people:

> *"Communism has an anti-natural and basically anti-economic quality. Its destruction does not distinguish error from truth, good from evil, justice from injustice. It does not care for history or the experience of humanity, for life or for the dignity of man. It is indifferent to the virtue of woman and to the affections of family life.*

---

43 https://www.en.wikipedia.org/wiki/Lend-Lease
44 <u>Time Runs Out</u> by Henry J. Taylor, 1942, p. 102

On the other hand, although Nazism differs from Communism in economic outlook, and this difference is too profound to be overlooked, in both cases the citizens lose their freedom and man loses God.

In both ideologies the Party is the State, to whose ends all citizens are subject. They exist only for the greatness of the State and for its glory. In each case, the State is its own reason for being." [45]

What else to look for when hunting for Fascism

While similar to socialism in some theories, terminologies and concomitant authoritarian rule, Fascism focuses on **conflict between nations and races** rather than class conflict. This is due to the fact that their are only two classes of people under Fascism, the one or the few in absolute power, and everyone else who are their vassals.

Free nations abhor tyrannical rule. Islam seeks the absolute control of all peoples of the world, and strives toward that end each and every day. As Winston Churchill once stated,

"The British and Americans do not war with races or governments as such. Tyranny, external or internal, is our foe, whatever trappings or disguises it wears, whatever language it speaks or perverts." [46]

---

45 <u>Time Runs Out</u> by Henry J. Taylor, 1942, p. 106
46 <u>Never Give In</u>: Challenging Words of Winston Churchill by Price & Walley, 1958, p. 16

Other traits of Fascism abound. They are described as romantic symbolism, a positive view of violence, promotion of masculinity, and mass mobilization of the populace. These definitions are given by Wikipedia, the online encyclopedia. Hatred is the very foundation of Fascism. If you mix racial hatred in, such as the Nazis and Muslims common hatred against Jewish people, a fire that can devour the entire planet is ignited. Hatred drives and sustains wicked, unscrupulous violence against innocents. Nazi Germany gives us one clear example of intense hatred in action:

> *"But Herr Hitler is not thinking only of stealing other people's territories, or flinging gobbets of them to his little confederate. I tell you truly what you must believe when I say this evil man, this monstrous abortion of hatred and defeat, is resolved on nothing less than the complete wiping out of the French nation..."* [47]

> *"These hopes that Hitler and his Nazis would become moderate and statesmanlike were illusory. Hatred of Jews was Hitler's whole motivation. His campaign against Jews became more and more murderous and demented right up to the time of his death."* [48]

At the head of this monster called Fascism are leaders who claim indisputable power. Opposition to or disagreement with its leaders is not tolerated. Complaints are also not allowed. This naturally dictates the absence of personal freedoms such as freedom of speech and of the press. Life is to be conducted in all facets, in adherence to the dictates of a Fascist nation's dictator(s).

---

47 <u>Their Finest Hour</u> by Winston Churchill, 1949, p. 510
48 <u>Blood, Tears and Folly</u> by Len Deighton, 1993, p. 136

Fascism is genuinely a revolutionary nationalism, with an obsessive preoccupation with humiliation or victimhood, in which Fascist leaders rally the masses to pursue redemptive violence against its perceived enemies, with the goals of internal cleansing and external expansion. In our day, anyone who listens to or watches world news events has heard militant Muslims declare "Islam is outraged" about this or that statement regarding the savage nature of Islam. Negative statements about Mohammed or the Islam religion are forbidden and warrant punishment, so say Muslim extremist groups and nations.

Resistance to and freedom from Fascism comes through either civil war within a country, or war between countries when the Fascist's aggression can no longer be tolerated. Millions of Germans paid with their lives for not resisting the rise and reign of Adolf Hitler's Nazi empire, which declared war on the entire western world. In the ensuing World War, Germany paid dearly. For example, a firestorm caused total destruction of Hamburg, Germany, from Allied bombings over a period of several days in which over 40,000 German people perished. A memorial plaque there in Hamburg reads in part, **"Remember these dead. Never again Fascism..."**

Fascist (Nazi) Germany initiated unprovoked acts of war, some declared and some undeclared, against free nations. Germany thus enslaved all of western Europe and parts of North Africa, over 300 million people, some for as long as nearly six years. The United States, Britain and their Allied powers, with great loss of life, defeated Fascist Germany and its Axis partners Italy and Japan in World War Two. Appeasement did not stop Hitler, only force of arms did!

ISLAM IS FASCISM

Islam claims to be a religion. But, Islam tries to dictate its belief system to every soul on the planet on a do or die basis. The more backward or third world the country, the greater the success has been, due to the inability of people to defend themselves against the violence that accompanies the spread of Islam. This is Fascism, not religion.

Noah Webster's 1828 Dictionary defines religion as godliness or real piety in practice, consisting in the performance of all known duties to God and to our fellow man, in obedience to divine command or from the love of God and his law.[49]

However, in the case of Islam, there is no semblance to propriety, love of fellow mankind, or even common decency. The opposite is true. Islam harbors hate, revenge, spite, terror, threat and murder. It also destroys the integrity of marriage and family through polygamy and sexual slavery, and thus further threatens the human decency and stability of any country in which Islam rules.

The term jihad or holy war is used in the Koran. Originally jihad meant "the expansion of Islam, by force if necessary." Practically speaking, it meant taking the political reins rather than killing the unbelievers. People of other faiths such as Christians and Jews were allowed to keep their own beliefs, but were taxed heavily by their Islamic rulers.[50]

---

49 American Dictionary of the English Language by Noah Webster, First Edition, 1828

50 American Jihad: The Terrorists Living Among Us by Steven Emerson, 2002, p. 223

Mohammed himself waged war against those who opposed him. He is counted as the founder of Islam, its "prophet." Yet, he was a military leader and political ruler. After his death in 632 A.D., factionalism developed among successor rulers in Islam, which has only degenerated into numerous sects of the "religion." Islam seeks world dominion, much the same as the Roman Catholic Church did under the Roman empire.

Through the centuries many warring factions of Islam have fought one another, claiming their leader to be the face of true Islam. The two largest Muslim sects, Sunni and Shia (Shi'ite) oppose each other. The three big players in Islam are: [51]

1) Muslim terrorist groups;
2) the Shia (Shi'ite) Muslim Islamic Republic of Iran;
3) the Sunni Muslim Saudi Arabia nation.

There are many terrorist groups of course. As of 2015, the I.S.I.S. group, now calling itself the Islamic State or I.S., is the most active. I.S. are Sunni Muslims, and are warring to take over the Mideast. But of the three players listed above, each one claims to be the only true and authentic form of Islam. Assassinations of would-be Islamic top dogs have been numerous.

Just as Germans were relegated to be pawns of their national government under Hitler, the followers of the cult of Islam have no choice but to follow Muslim rites and practices or face death. This is because what the government dictates, which operates

---

51 <u>The Crisis of Islam</u> by Bernard Lewis, 2003, p. 138

coincidentally as a religion, is what everyone who wants to continue living will do. A good explanation of the political climate that fosters such goings on is seen under Hitler from 1933 to 1945:

> *"Once the democratic concept of a government belonging to the people is displaced by a State or State-idol to whom the people belong, through blind faith or obedience, and the State alone decides what is right and what is wrong, human life inevitably becomes cheap. If a people have no regard for their own rights, it follows that they have no respect for the rights of others."* [52]

Islamic sects or factions are at war with other factions of Islam **and** the entire non-Muslim world! It is a declared war, which they call jihad or holy war. It is not simply individual acts of terror by Muslims as the news media would have people believe. These acts of violence are all part of the war declared and ongoing in the name of their mystic god. Muslim terrorists often shout "Allah Akbar" which means "god is great," as they commit murder and other terrorist acts. (If he is so great, one wonders, why does he need the help of humans to destroy puny human beings?)

To non-Muslims, God is not thought to be connected today with mass murder or violence, nor ordering others to commit unprovoked, premeditated murder. But the automatons of Islam are so thoroughly indoctrinated with the hatred of others and their own superiority that violence and killing of innocents seems fully justified in the name of their god.

---

52 <u>This Must Not Happen Again! The Black Book of Fascist Horror</u> by Clark Kinnaird, 1945, p. 13

The warfare that Fascist groups wage is not only militaristic, it is also psychological warfare against all perceived enemies. Such was the case in Hitler's Germany, and the Nazi description of psychological warfare there fits like a glove on today's Islamic modus operandi:

> *"Psychologically, the leadership principle revolves around Der Fuehrer who delegates authority to sub-leaders in the form of a person-to-person mandate. The personal interrelationships between Der Fuehrer (Adolf Hitler) and his followers (Germanic people everywhere in the world) is the psychological basis of the whole Nazi political system. To establish and solidify this personal interrelationship, the Nazis apply all weapons of psychological warfare (indoctrination, propaganda, terror, intimidation) to the German people themselves."* [53]

Fascists despise weakness in their enemies, and if it is perceived that the enemy of Fascism lacks aggression to meet Fascist threats, trouble follows such as the example that Germany in World War Two gives us in hatred toward America:

> *"They despise us as they have come to despise the English, who at the most critical moment in the history of the modern world fled in panic before Adolf Hitler's threats, and the events of the last four years have clearly proven that both the Nazis and the Fascists will attack anyone whom they suspect of 'moral weakness', for such weakness, especially in the eyes of the Nazis, deserves to be answered only by violence and force of arms."* [54]

---

53 <u>German Psychological Warfare</u> by Ladislas Fargo 1942, p. 35
54 <u>Our Battle</u> by Hendrik Willem Van Loon 1939, p. 18

The world has seen the impoverishments, the suffering, the hostage-taking, the executions, the battles and the civilian casualties from Fascist aggression by Germany, Italy and Japan in World War Two. Yet today, a similar Fascist force against free people exists under the name Islam. It threatens and carries out acts of violence, kidnapping, bombings and death to its adversaries. It is a strange way indeed of convincing a person to believe in a supreme being.

Nonetheless, ongoing, coordinated, multi-national action is not taken to stop the spread of Islamic violence around the globe except in limited instances pursuing terrorists who commit mass killings. As a result, millions of Muslims and non-Muslims are fleeing for their lives from Syria, Iraq and elsewhere, for fear of the terrorist group I.S. (Islamic State). This huge influx of Muslim refugees into western Europe also serves the future purposes of militant Islam, as those Muslims and their offspring can be radicalized later to conduct Islamic jihad.

Islamic nations do not directly declare war for the most part, with the exception of the Islamic Republic of Iran. Instead, certain rogue Islamic nations train and send out their cowardly, masked terrorists to conduct guerrilla warfare against civilians and governments alike. One simply has to mention "9-11" or "Benghazi" and most everyone knows of what those are in reference. Islamic Fascism is an undeclared war, in that no formal declaration of war is usually given to another nation. But it is a declared war on non-Islamic peoples by the "religion" of Islam, which further identifies Islam for what it is **not**--a religion or aspiration for right ways or for loving ones neighbor as oneself.

Fascism by a simple definition is the force of armed thugs who happen to carry the force of law, because the leaders happen to be the leaders of a nation State--usually militant, Islamic dictatorships. In the Islamic world, there is no room for individual choice. The religion of the State is Islam and Islamic beliefs are the dictates of law. Islamic dictators carry their religion to work with them, which makes them dangerous.

When government is run by the staunch dictates of Islam, watch out. Would you like to live there? The New York Times reported in May, 2015 that the Saudi Arabian government had advertised for job seekers there, because eight vacancies existed for executioners due to an increase in beheadings and a "...scarcity of qualified swordsmen..."[55]

Many of the same violent tactics used by Nazi Germany in World War Two are exhibited regularly in Islamic life, and in terrorist attacks in various places around the globe in our day. This treatise examines many examples of Fascist behavior from history, in the following pages, to illustrate more fully what Fascism is and what Fascism dictates.

OTHER FASCISTS DO EXIST

There are other Fascist regimes on the planet, such as North Korea and Cuba. While both are dangerous, the threats that either one have made against other nations of the world have been for the most part just talk. But within these two countries, the people are virtual automatons of the all powerful State. The next section, Chapter Two, includes a look at North Korea.

---

55 The Complete Infidels Guide to ISIS by Robert Spencer, 2015, p.135

CHAPTER 2

Fascism makes
its own laws

———

FASCISM OF YESTERYEAR

THE EXTREMISM REPRESENTED BY FASCISM demands its own set of laws and edicts. Adolf Hitler became Chancellor of Germany on January 30, 1933. Then he set his brand of Fascist rule in motion through an arson fire in Germany's national parliament building on February 27, 1933, which was said to be started by Communists. The truth was Hitler's own forces had started the fire as a pretense to expand his power.

Hitler subsequently arrested and imprisoned one hundred members of Germany's national legislative body called the Reichstag, and coerced the remaining members of that body to give Hitler personally, absolute power for a crisis, intended to be temporary. But Hitler made that temporary power permanent and absolute through intimidation, violence, lies and terror. Hitler's murderous regime continued for twelve years:

"The so-called law suspended all the fundamental constitutional guarantees of personal liberty, freedom of conscience

and of opinion...Today, I can no longer hesitate: I say that all the "laws," all the decrees enacted by the National Socialist government, are illegal. In law, they are null and void, since they are based upon a crime and an abuse of confidence. Hitler achieved power by engineering a political combination...The burning of the Reichstag is the criminal act by which he perjured himself and usurped the power to rule."[56]

Ruthlessness is a central theme of Fascism, which abolishes governments in territories it conquers, and murders anyone who might be a threat to centralized, dictatorial rule. Subsequently, the dogma or set of beliefs by which the victorious Fascism operates, becomes the law! A real world example when and where it occurred will be detailed after one author's brief explanation of how this comes to pass:

"For any gigantic regimented State generates within itself tensions and aggressive movements which, in the long run, become uncontrollable. Power is effective, internally and externally, if it is exerted with an always increasing momentum. But it is conducive to peace only for a short time. It is a failure as a basis for anything but war."[57]

In mid-August, 1939, Germany and Russia negotiated a treaty of non-aggression in which they agreed not to attack each other, but to remain at peace. Part of that agreement stipulated that the country of Poland, which is situated between the two countries, was to be abolished as a nation and the territory of Poland split in

---

56 <u>I Paid Hitler</u> by Fritz Thyssen, 1941, p. 67
57 <u>Men and Power</u> by Henry J. Taylor, 1946, p. 16

half, with the east half annexed to Russia, and the west half becoming part of Germany.

The aftermath of this agreement between two Fascist nations, Germany and Russia, had numerous negative connotations and consequences, namely:

(1) Germany wasted no time in taking their slice of the pie. Less than two weeks later (September 1, 1939), Nazi armies invaded Poland, bombing its cities, imprisoning and exterminating its intelligentsia, deporting more than one and a half million Poles to Germany as forced laborers, confining all Jews to ghettos or concentration camps, and locking up 400,000 Poles as prisoners of war. The country was virtually gutted. Estimates of Poles shot by firing squads or hung from gallows in short order, without any trial, was 85,000 people.[58] Tens of thousands of Germans were relocated to re-populate Poland, taking over land and property that cost them nothing.

(2) Russia, conversely, knowing that war with their mortal enemy Germany was inevitable--despite their no-war agreement with Germany--crossed into eastern Poland and presented themselves as liberators to the Poles on the same date, September 1, 1939. They proceeded to order, at gunpoint, Polish Army troops fleeing in disorder from the Nazi troops, to lay down their weaponry, and subsequently shipped them off to Russia by the trainload, to be united with their own Russian army.[59]

---

58 <u>Underground Europe</u> by Curt Riess, 1942, p. 197
59 <u>Story of a Secret State</u> by Jan Karski, 1944, p. 13

(3) On September 3, 1939, two days after Germany invaded Poland, Britain, France, Australia and New Zealand declared war on Germany. The rape of Poland basically delineated the start of World War Two, as free nations had to declare their intent to stop Hitler and his Nazis from the takeover of Europe. (Take note: A future declaration of war against militant Islam is imminent.)

Fascism of today

North Korea

North Korea today is under a Fascist dictatorship now headed by the grandson of its founder. By agreement between the Allied powers, Korea was split into two separate nations, North and South Korea, at the end of World War Two. North Korea, north of the 38th parallel, came into being as a protectorate-nation of the Soviet Union at the end of World War Two. The United States was given the rest of the Korean peninsula, south of the 38th parallel, to disarm the Japanese present there, and to help establish a new government. The split of this country into protectorate territories did not suit the North Koreans or their Russian handlers, who refused to participate in free elections for the entire peninsula.

Then on June 25, 1950, the North Korean army numbering about 100,000 men, after a massive artillery barrage, began an across-the-border invasion of South Korea (below the 38th parallel). This was the start of the Korean War. North Koreans are taught by their dictator that the war started when South Korea invaded

North Korea![60] The United Nations Security Council called for an end to the aggression and a withdrawal of North Korean troops, which did not happen.

The Korean War was a seesaw affair, with North Korea's army at one point capturing the entire Korean peninsula with the aid of an estimated 200,000 Red Chinese army troops from Communist China.[61] But with superior fire power, jet fighters and a surprise amphibious landing at Inchon by General Douglas MacArthur's forces, the United States armed forces with some help from other nations, drove the enemy far back into North Korea. Most of the armaments used by the North Korean Armed Forces were of Russian manufacture.

An armistice, nothing more than a cease-fire agreement, was signed on July 27, 1953 after three years of war. This was just four months after the death of Soviet dictator Joseph Stalin. Fascist aggression, in this case North Korean, guided and aided by the Soviet Union, is always the same. It is generally unannounced violent revolution or war, in the name of the Fascist empire which rules the aggressor nation.[62]

Naturally, because of the Soviet oversight, North Korea developed as a Communist dictatorship under a man named Kim Il-sung. The official name is the Democratic People's Republic of Korea. The country calls itself a self-reliant Socialist state, but could be hardly considered to be self-reliant, in the face of state-run

---

60 Escape from Camp 14 by Blaine Harden, 2012, p. 161
61 Mandate for Change by Dwight D. Eisenhower, 1963, p. 176
62 Korean War Almanac by Harry Summers Jr, 1990, pp. 17-33

collective farms and enterprises that have left the country short of food, with hundreds of thousands of civilians dying from famine. "Internationally, however, it is considered a totalitarian dictatorship."[63]

Here is how the worldwide organization called Amnesty International describes North Korea:

> *"North Korea is in a category of its own when it comes to human rights violations. It is a totalitarian state where tens of thousands of people are enslaved and tortured. All forms of expression are repressed and anyone attempting to assert their rights is crushed. In North Korea, where failing to show sufficient reverence for the country's leaders is a serious offense, no one is safe from arrest and imprisonment."*[64]

The population of North Korea is about 25 million. Because of Fascist paranoia, the country has a total of nearly 10 million military personnel, with an active army of 1,210,000 men, making it the fourth largest standing army in the world.[65] The army is kept on a constant state of alert due to the typical paranoia of Fascist empires. There have been tensions because of minor hostile military action by North Korea off and on since the Korean War ended in a truce, with no armistice or permanent peace agreement to date.

In January, 1968, the United States Navy ship the USS Pueblo supposedly trespassed into North Korean waters and was boarded

---

63 https://www.en.wikipedia.org/wiki/North_Korean_cult of personality
64 http: www.amnesty.org.uk/issues/north-korea
65 https://www.en.wikipedia.org/wiki/North_Korean_cult of personality

and captured by the North Koreans. The crew was interned, interrogated and tortured. The USS Pueblo remains in the hands of the North Koreans because of cowardly American leadership. The USS Pueblo is used as a public museum to persuade the people of North Korea of the evil intentions of the weak United States. Any offers of trade or the lessening of tensions between the two Korean nations are usually rebuffed, and always regarded with suspicion by the North Korean dictator.

North Korea's present dictator is Kim Jong-un, the grandson of North Korea's founder. The country poses an ongoing threat to South Korea, Japan, the Philippines, and even the United States due to the fact that North Korea possesses both long range rocketry and nuclear warheads on its missiles.

It is estimated by neighboring South Korea, that North Korea currently has over 150,000 people enslaved in prison work camps. Shin In Geun was a political prisoner, born in one of these North Korean camps, called Camp 14. Shin's father and mother had been cast into this forced labor camp because other distant family members of Shin were perceived to be in opposition to the Kim dynasty. As is usually the case, entire families and their relatives are subsequently cast into these prison-like labor camps.

The North Korean forced labor camps are in every detail akin to Nazi concentration camps of an earlier day. The prisoners work untold hours, are underfed and poorly clothed. Hunger forces them to eat whatever they can lay hold of, even if it is rats. Prisoners are beaten and tortured regularly by sadistic guards. Women prisoners are raped repeatedly by guards, but then if found pregnant they are mysteriously never seen again. Prisoners are forced in daily sessions, to confess their short-comings in their day's labor, whether that labor is feeding hogs raised for feeding the army, or sewing army uniforms. Executions of prisoners are a regular occurrence, by hanging or firing squad, for violating any rules. Watching the camp executions are compulsory for all prisoners.[66]

North Korea is virtually sealed off from the eyes of outsiders. The few visitors that are allowed into the country from time to time are ushered about under very close guard, and are not allowed to speak with anyone but high government officials which were agreed upon in advance to be addressed. This is typical of oppressed peoples living under Fascism. One Fascist empire, the Soviet Union, has bred another Fascist empire, North Korea.

In stark contrast, The Republic of Korea, as South Korea is officially known, developed as a democratic nation under American occupation after World War Two, once the Japanese were disarmed and expelled. Its national government has an executive, legislative and judicial branch just as the United States does.

South Korea today is one of the richest nations in the world.[67] With a population twice that of North Korea, South Korea's economy is 38 times larger than North Korea, [68] making South Korea the 13th largest economy in the world, in terms of gross national product.[69] Whether a country becomes free or Fascist

---

66 Escape from Camp 14 by Blaine Harden, 2012, pp. 4-8
67 The Black Book of the American Left by D. Horowitz, 2013, p. 247
68 Escape from Camp 14 by Blaine Harden, 2012, p. 170
69 https://en.wikipedia.org/wiki/South_Korea

does make a difference! North Korea, under Fascist rule, cannot even feed its own people, while a well-fed army is kept in constant readiness for war.

JAPAN

Japan was a Fascist empire under militaristic leaders in the 1930's. The emperor, Hirohito, was considered a god and worshipped as such. His aura was considered so heavenly that beginning in 1936 it became unlawful for Japanese citizens to look at Emperor Hirohito, as they bowed in his presence or before his royal palace in Tokyo. Violators were arrested by police.[70]

Japan's unprovoked attack on the U.S. Naval base at Pearl Harbor, Hawaii in December, 1941, brought the United States into World War Two. Japan conducted its war efforts with reckless abandon, and treated prisoners of war in extremely cruel and inhuman fashion. Over 28% of all Allied WW2 prisoners of war died while in Japanese captivity, the majority from poor diet and disease. [71] Many were decapitated. (By contrast, only 4% of Allied prisoners of war held in Germany died in captivity.[72])

At the end of World War Two, the United States became the sole occupying power in the country of Japan. America poured $400 million per year in U.S. funds into the relief and rebuilding of Japan.[73] Elections were held, and for the first time in its history, women

---

70 Japan at War, by Col. John Elting, 1980, p. 87
71 Coast Artillery Journal by U.S. Army Artillery, Mar-Apr 1946, p. 42
72 Prisoners of War by Ronald Bailey, 1981, p. 13
73 The Aftermath: Asia by Col. John Elting, 1983, p. 54

were given the right to vote in the new democratic government established. Rule by an Emperor ended, though Hirohito was allowed to continue as a figure head. Under Douglas MacArthur's leadership, the Japanese parliament, called the Diet, passed the Farm Land Reform Act in 1946, which mandated the sale of five million acres of agricultural land to the government. Then in turn, the government sold the land to the former sharecropping tenants at modest prices, with payment due over a thirty year period.

By 1954, there was no need for any further aid to Japan. The economy boomed. Cities, homes and shops were rebuilt. In 2012, Japan ranked as the third largest economy in the world after the United States and China, though Japan has just 127 million people.[74] Japan is another example of the huge difference it makes in what political ideology and structure a nation's government exists, and of what freedoms are granted to that nation's people.

Islamic Fascism

Islam has become entrenched in the seat of governments--with Islam the only religion thereafter tolerated--in numerous countries through violence and the threat of violence. This is the beginning of an oppressed people. This is the end of freedom where this happens. Who is to stop them? The United Nations certainly will not, being one unending argument between free nations and Communist (Fascist) ones.

---

74 https://www.en.wikipedia.org/wiki/Japan#Demographics

With the Fascist Islamic ideology, existing under the guise of religion, comes the well established brand of tyranny for the unfortunate subjects of a country via something called "Sharia Law":

" The introduction of Sharia is a longstanding goal for Islamist movements globally, including in Western countries, but attempts to impose Sharia have been accompanied by controversy, violence, and even warfare. Most countries do not recognize Sharia; however, some countries in Asia, Africa and Europe recognize Sharia and use it as the basis for divorce, inheritance and other personal affairs of their Islamic population. In Britain, the Muslim Arbitration Tribunal makes use of Sharia family law to settle disputes, and this limited adoption of Sharia is controversial.

The concept of crime, judicial process, justice and punishment embodied in Sharia is different from that of secular law. The differences between Sharia and secular laws have led to an on-going controversy as to whether Sharia is compatible with secular democracy, freedom of thought, and women's rights." [75]

ISLAMIC RULE MEANS GOVERNMENT AND RELIGION ARE SYNONYMOUS

Fascism brings enslavement. Islam brings enslavement. Today, does the world see freedom of choice when Islamists bearing automatic weapons and swords show up on the scene somewhere in the world? No, we see violence, and an attempt to impose Islamic

---

75 Sharia Law by Wikipedia, the Online Encyclopedia, Wikimedia Foundation, 2014

tyranny and slavery on the populace, and the denial of basic human rights. Muslims are frankly not at all concerned with world opinion of what they do.

Mosques are constructed around the globe, largely funded by Saudi Arabian oil profits.[76] In America today elaborate, very costly mosques are certainly not being paid for by Moslems present in America today, seeing there are less than three million Muslims in the United States.

But if Islam can, through immigration and high birth rates of Muslims, become a significant enough portion of the American population, then it can begin to impose its own Islamic Sharia Law in America via political power. Sharia law constitutes tyranny and arbitrary totalitarian rule by Islamic clerics, according to their own interpretation of the Koran. This must not happen in the land of the free, and the home of the (formerly) brave.

Consider the country of Iran, officially known as the Islamic Republic of Iran. Ayatollah Khomeini, an Islamic cleric, took political control of Iran as the "Supreme Leader" after the Islamic revolution of 1979. The present population of Iran is 78 million people, who are all automatons of Iran's supreme dictator. Tens of thousands of opponents of the new regime including Marxists and various ethnic groups in areas such as Kurdistan, Khuzestan, Balochistan were executed subsequent to the 1979 Iranian revolution.

---

76 The Black Book of the American Left by D. Horowitz, 2013, p. 397

In Iran, a Guardian Council of twelve men oversee the Iranian Parliament. The Council interprets the constitution and may veto Parliament. If a law is deemed incompatible with the constitution or Sharia (Islamic law), it is referred back to Parliament for revision.[77]

According to a news report of the British Broadcasting Corporation, Muslim clerics exercise considerable power over Muslim societies.[78] The same news article, dated July 14, 2015, reported that President George Bush had declared Iran to be part of an "axis of evil" in 2002, because of its direct connections to Shia (Shi'ite) Islamic terrorism.

How dangerous is Iran? consider the Iran Travel Warning published by the U.S. State Department, updated on August 5, 2015:

"The Department of State warns U.S. citizens to carefully consider the risks of travel to Iran...The Iranian government continues to repress some minority religious and ethnic groups, including Christians, Baha'i, Arabs, Kurds, Azeris, and others. Consequently, some areas within the country where these minorities reside, including the Baluchistan border area near Pakistan and Afghanistan, the Kurdish northwest of the country, and areas near the Iraqi border, remain unsafe. Iranian authorities have detained and harassed U.S. citizens, particularly those of Iranian origin. Former Muslims who have converted to other religions,

---

77 https://en.wikipedia.org/wiki/Iran#Religion
78 http://www.bbc.com/news/world-middle-east-14541327

religious activists, and persons who encourage Muslims to convert are subject to arrest and prosecution."[79]

Of the two dozen or so nations which are currently on the Do Not Travel List of the State Department, warning U.S. citizens not to travel there, nearly all are militant, Islamic dictatorships including Iraq, Iran, Libya, Lebanon, Tunisia, Algeria, Yemen, Senegal, Mali, Mauritania, Niger, Chad, Sudan, Eritrea, Pakistan, and Afghanistan. Travel to other countries with Muslim unrest, violence and/or the increased risk of terrorist violence are also included, such as India.

The foreign travel warning list shows an interesting statistic. Of the 1.6 billion Muslims in the world, countries where Americans are warned not to travel because of Muslim terrorism possess 920 million or nearly 60% of the world's Muslim population.[80] The travel warning list shows the direct correlation between countries that are primarily or exclusively Islamic, and the danger of falling victim to Islamic terrorism.

Here is a partial listing quoted from the U.S. State Department's Worldwide Travel Warnings dated July 29, 2015. Notice the names of Islamic terrorist organizations mentioned in just this short portion of the travel advisory:

"Kidnappings and hostage events involving U.S. citizens have become increasingly prevalent as ISIL, al-Qa'ida and

---

79 http://travel.state.gov/content/passports/english/alertswarnings/iran-travel-warning.html#

80 http://travel.state.gov/content/passports/english/alertswarnings.html

*its affiliates have increased attempts to finance their opera-
tions through kidnapping for ransom operations. U.S. citizens
have been kidnapped and murdered by members of terrorist
and violent extremist groups. ISIL, al-Qa'ida in the Arabian
Peninsula (AQAP) and al-Qa'ida in the Islamic Maghreb
(AQIM) are particularly effective with kidnapping for ransom and are using ransom money to fund the range of their
activities.*

*Extremists may elect to use conventional or non-conven-
tional weapons, and target both official and private interests.
Examples of such targets include high-profile sporting events,
residential areas, business offices, hotels, clubs, restaurants,
places of worship, schools, public areas, shopping malls, and
other tourist destinations both in the United States and abroad
where U.S. citizens gather in large numbers, including during
holidays."* [81]

The world is in grave danger from militant Islam, as even the U.S.
State Department acknowledges. The problem will not go away by
itself.

In summary, when the religion of Islam rules nations, the savage laws of the Islamic religion and the whims of its dictatorial
leaders translate into life under Fascism. Conformance to Islamic
laws govern every facet of life, and result in polygamy, the subjugation of women and the outlawing of any practices or lifestyle
deemed incompatible with the Islamic Sharia Law.

---

81 http://travel.state.gov/content/passports/english/alertswarnings/worldwide-
caution.html

Speaking against the alleged prophet of Islam, Mohammed, or even drawing a picture or likeness of Mohammed, brings a sentence of death. (Speaking against Der Fuehrer Adolf Hitler in Nazi Germany brought the identical reward for the offender.)

In the world of children we have bullies, that boss, threaten and injure other children. In the world of adults today, we continue to have Fascist bullies and tyrants. Hitler deceived himself by the illusion that Germany's future involved the domination of Europe and the world. Likewise, many Muslim terrorist groups and nations are deceived by their prideful and greedy expectations of ruling the whole world.

CHAPTER 3

Fascists Paranoia and Propaganda

(kill our enemies before they kill us)

————

WHEN FASCIST LEADERS STRIKE OUT in force against enemies, they use propaganda to boldly lie. Their portrayals of events declare their very existence to be a dangerous and violent paranoid force. In the case of Nazi Germany during World War Two, foreign journalists in Berlin were shown propaganda newsreels of the devastation given out by German bombs after Germany invaded peaceful and peaceable Holland and Belgium:

> *"Pictures of the German army smashing through Belgium and Holland. Some of the more destructive work of German bombs and shells was shown. Towns laid waste, dead soldiers and horses lying around, and the earth and mortar flying when a shell or bomb hit."* [82]

> *"The paranoid's sense of justice--one rule for me, another for the rest of the world--is classically exemplified in the attitude of*

<hr>

[82] <u>Berlin Diary</u> by William Shirer, 1941, p. 342

a German announcer showing uncensored newsreels at a press conference Shirer attended. Pictures of devastated Holland and Belgium inspired him to shout: **'thus do we deal death and destruction on our enemies!'** *Pictures of damage from English bombs at Freiburg, Germany, brought forth a righteously indignant* **'Thus do our brutal and unscrupulous enemies bomb and kill and murder innocent German children.'** *"[83]*

William Shirer worked as a news correspondent for American newspaper and radio outlets during the entire Second World War. He lived and worked in Hitler's Germany for the first six years of Hitler's twelve years in power. Shirer's first hand news accounts of events in Hitler's empire were not flattering and put his very life in danger because he evaded and skirted censorship by Germany's Propaganda Ministry wherever possible.

Here is what Shirer stated upon his relocation to Geneva, Switzerland in 1938, to continue covering events in Germany but allowing his wife to dwell in the safety of Switzerland:

"*We are glad to be leaving Berlin. To sum up these last three years: Personally, they have not been unhappy ones, though the shadow of Nazi fanaticism, sadism, persecution, regimentation, terror, brutality, suppression, militarism and preparation for war has hung over all our lives, like a dark, brooding cloud that never clears.*"[84]

---

83 <u>Is Germany Incurable?</u> by Richard Brickner M.D. 1943, p. 151
84 <u>Berlin Diary</u> by William Shirer, 1941, p. 33

Shirer relates the tense atmosphere created by censorship in Germany in October, 1940, as he traveled back and forth from Geneva to Berlin to cover Hitler's expanding Fascist empire:

> *"The new instructions of both the military and the political censors are that they cannot allow me to say anything which might create an unfavourable impression for Nazi Germany in the United States. Moreover, the new restrictions about reporting air attacks force you either to give a completely false picture of them or to omit mention of them altogether. I usually do the latter, but it is almost as dishonest as the former. In short, you can no longer report the war or conditions in Germany as they are. You cannot call the Nazis 'Nazis' or an invasion an 'invasion.' You are reduced to re-broadcasting the official communiques, which are lies, and which any automaton can do."* [85]

What is propaganda? Synonyms for propaganda are advertising, fear mongering, bold lying and psychological warfare. Most people know how powerful a message becomes through repetition. Advertising messages are propaganda aimed at motivating a person to make a purchase or acquire a habit. The advertisements are not always true! But the repetition of the message, as in advertising, is very successful in motivating behavior.

Propaganda in the form of lying is used to prejudice and mislead an audience as to the truth of actual events. It is a well documented fact that Hitler staged the supposed invasion of Germany by Poland prior to Germany's armed forces attack on Poland on September 1, 1939. Germany took 12 or 13 Polish criminals out

---

85 Ibid., p.543

of a German prison, forced them to attire themselves in Polish army uniforms, then killed them and placed their bodies in array with weaponry on German soil near the Polish border.[86] Carefully photographed and beamed to the world was the falsehood that Poland had attacked Germany, and Germany could stand for no more such aggression, but acted to protect Germany's sovereignty. This is first rate paranoid propaganda! (As with Islamic terrorism today, it is purported to be the victim's fault that the violence was perpetrated.)

Propaganda is used in subtly advancing war aims. Psychological warfare has been around for well over one hundred years. What the Nazi Germans did in World War Two was to improve its technique to whitewash their violent aggression:

> *"A not unimportant aspect of psychological warfare is the weapon of scapegoatism, a device as old as history itself. The Germans borrowed heavily from history in developing their scapegoat technique as a method of taking the blame of gross bestiality away from themselves and as a convenient means of concealing their real motives in the plan for world conquest."* [87]

Nazi Germany projected their own behavior on their adversaries. It was a simple process. German propaganda announced that surrounding countries had behaved in an aggressive manner toward Germany itself, or German inhabitants of a neighboring country, such as Poland. This alleged behavior of neighbors justified, Hitler declared, Germany's acts of war against all of Europe. This is

---

86 <u>The Rise and Fall of the Third Reich</u> by William Shirer, 1960, p. 520
87 <u>Paper Bullets</u> by Leo Margolin 1946, p. 21

paranoia. The truth was, no neighboring country was making <u>any</u> acts of aggression toward Germany <u>at all</u>!

> *"All people who possess strong paranoid tendencies are potential sources of danger to their fellows, especially since, once their fundamental premises are granted, they are clever and logical in their ruthlessness. Individual paranoids produce disastrous effects on the people among whom they live. Paranoids in position of power produce effects even more disastrous on very large groups. Through lack of any knowledge of paranoia, friends and families of individual paranoids and statesmen dealing with paranoids in high places invariably react in precisely the way calculated to make the situation worse."* [88]

Neville Chamberlain, Prime Minister of England, found out the truth of that fact with a trip to Berlin to appease Adolf Hitler with the "peace in our time" agenda he brought for Mr. Hitler. However, he returned to England not only unable to secure peace, but with new German demands upon England to boot. [89]

> *"Paranoids do not bluff. They merely refrain from shooting until, according to their irrational values, the despicable or presumptuous behavior of others forces them to pull the trigger"...."The paranoid has no mental facilities for understanding an unsympathetic outsider's attitude toward his successive demands, each prefaced by a broken pledge. To him,*

88 <u>Is Germany Incurable?</u> by Richard Brickner, M.D., 1943, p. 60-61
89 <u>Deadline</u> by Pierre Lazareff, 1942, p. 187

> *each fresh demand is even better justified than the last, be-*
> *cause its emotional content is higher."* [90]

Because of Hitler's demands that injustices done to Germans in Czechoslovakia be righted, Hitler proceeded to threaten the Czech nation with invasion by German armies, unless the Sudeten area of northern Bohemia was annexed to Germany. Negotiators in this matter were instructed to request ever-wider concessions from Czechoslovakia "but never to be satisfied." [91] The Czechoslovakian nation was basically handed to Germany by negotiations with Allied nations without firing a shot. And ironically, Czechoslovakia manned an army which was fully capable of stopping Hitler's Germany at that point in time. But paranoids cannot be appeased and Germany was not appeased!

Justice in the eyes of Nazi Germany, for alleged wrongs against Germany was extreme, violent acts of aggression. For example, the city of Copenhagen, Denmark was bombed one early morning by German planes, without warning, and without a declaration of war. Germany claimed that Denmark's leaders had refused to cooperate with the idea of German military occupation of their country. Occupation, it was said, was in order to protect them from attack by Britain and France! That was a big lie. Nazi propagandists then announced to the world "only a few hundred people" who resisted the German occupation had died. In truth, the death toll there from total destruction by aerial bombardment of nearly one and a half square miles of the central city of Copenhagen, was

90 <u>Is Germany Incurable?</u> by Richard Brickner, M.D., 1943, p. 273
91 <u>Master of Spies</u> by General Frantisek Moravec, 1975, p. 108

over 60,000 innocent Danes killed. And 28,000 buildings were destroyed.[92] Some protection plan!

Many other examples of Fascist violence were perpetrated by Nazi Germany. One author wrote:

> *"To me, the most frightful example is Rotterdam. This great commercial city has always stood in close relation to Germany, and many buildings there were German property. What has been perpetrated in the destruction of that city is indescribable. I cannot imagine that the French would ever have destroyed Strassburg in so ruthless a manner. All this simply shows the urge to get ahead quickly; that is the reason for spreading terror on every side. No German in future will be able to show himself in the world without shame."* [93]

FASCIST FOLLOWERS BECOME ROBOTS THROUGH PROPAGANDA

Followers of Fascist ideologies as a group, are educated by their leaders to be distrustful of others, and to develop definite tendencies of paranoia. In time, they become robot followers of violence and evil. Yet their guilt for the eventual conducting of war and shedding of blood cannot be erased. As in the case of Germany, where its people followed Hitler's Fascist National Socialism (Nazi) party:

> *"There is a point at which the seduced become guilty. There is a borderline that may not be crossed by those who would*

---

92 <u>This is the Enemy</u> by Frederick Oechsner 1942, p. 335
93 <u>I Paid Hitler</u> by Fritz Thyssen, 1941, p. 277

disclaim responsibility. What is happening in Poland, in Czechoslovakia, in France, in Norway, in all the occupied territories, is not Hitler's work alone. It is not merely the work of a few thousand Gestapo agents. It is not even the sole achievement of 500,000 or 1,000,000 fanatic Nazis. Millions of Germans have a share in it, misled in the beginning perhaps, but steeped in guilt long since."[94]

Fascists, being paranoid among other unsavory characteristics, are certain in their minds that the world is against them and plotting their destruction. As one author, who met and spoke with Adolf Hitler face to face on a number of occasions, later wrote about Adolf Hitler:

"Hitler always said Germany was being 'encircled' and that the freedom and lives of every man and woman in Germany were at stake. Germany wanted nothing that was not her due. But others wanted Germany."[95]

Psychological warfare used on the battlefield itself is a powerful force. It has been used in many forms by opponents in war. Germany's Marshall Hindenburg spoke about such flyers used against Germany in the First World War:

"The enemy hopes that many a field-gray soldier will send home the leaflet which has innocently fluttered down from the air. At home it will pass from hand to hand and be discussed at the beer table, in families, in the drawing-room, in

---

94 <u>Underground Europe</u> by Curt Riess 1942, p. 294
95 <u>Men and Power</u> by Henry J. Taylor 1946, p.191

factories and in the street. Unsuspectingly many thousands consume the poison." [96]

Some Allied leaflets in World War Two were anything but subtle. One declared "I Surrender: Use This As Safe Conduct Pass To American Soldiers." Another Allied message asked "Where is Hitler?" on leaflets dropped by Allied planes over Germany in World War Two. This type of demoralizing propaganda worked.[97]

Psychological warfare tactics were used by the Nazi party in Germany to come into power in the nation's government. Their tactics included:[98]

1. Finding fault with the Constitution
2. Abusing national symbols such as the flag
3. Mass meetings
4. Wearing of forbidden clothing
5. Obstructing law enforcement agencies
6. Intimidation by violent acts and threat of violence
7. Murder to instill fear in the populace

All of these tactics have been utilized by militant Muslims here in the United States as they seek the eventual takeover of America. The entire non-Islamic world is perceived to be against the religion of Mohammed, and therefore as the enemies of Islam literally hundreds of cases of beheadings, bombings, hijackings, kidnappings and shootings come to light in the news.

---

96 <u>Paper Bullets</u> by Leo Margolin, 1946, p. 18
97 Ibid., p. 50
98 <u>German Psychological Warfare</u> by Ladislas Farago, 1942, p. 135

But if an Allied drone should strike a known terrorist leader somewhere in the world, Muslims lay claim to an American drone strike on a school full of children--which the terrorist purposely dwell among to criminalize the opposition. Such actions point to the paranoid nature of Islam. Terrorist acts including military style attacks contribute toward the hoped-for surrender of America to Islamic rule. If so, the Islamists have misjudged America. American history proves that Americans are willing to fight for their freedoms against their enemies. But the wake up call to the real threat is overdue.

CHAPTER 4

Megalomania

———

It has been said that power corrupts. Among Thomas Jefferson's writings for our new American republic, was an essay written in 1778 espousing the education of Americans about the very notion of the tendency of government power to grow to the place where freedoms are curtailed or endangered:

> *"Whereas it appeareth that however certain forms of government are better calculated than others to protect individuals in the free exercise of their natural rights, and are at the same time themselves better guarded against degeneracy, yet experience hath shown, that even under the best forms, those entrusted with power have, in time, and by slow operations, perverted it into tyranny;..."* [99]

A further warning by all must be taken when paranoid rulers of nations display grandiose portrayals of themselves by making demands lacking common sense. One example is the treaty demanded by Iran from the United States of America. The foolish United States government has agreed to a very lopsided agreement

[99] The Political Writings of Thomas Jefferson by Merrill Peterson, 1993, p. 44

virtually safeguarding Iran as they develop nuclear weapons which the treaty was intended to forestall. Demands are always exaggerated and one sided. Simply stated:

> *"The paranoid is the megalomaniac, treating his environment exclusively as device for his own aggrandizement and glorification. Grandiose mystic notions of the cosmos that nobody can refute because they have no basis in everyday life crop up in him, huge, world-embracing thoughts that make the thinker feel as big as the universe. He often develops a belief in Destiny or The Wave of the Future or a personal divine mission or an exclusive personal right to satiation of all his desires and ambitions--although he is by definition incapable of satisfaction in any triumph. Others' failures to cooperate...give him a persecution complex."* [100]

Wikipedia defines megalomania as a psychopathological condition seen in tyrannical rulers and others, characterized by delusional fantasies of power, relevance, omnipotence and inflated self-esteem. It was previously referred to as narcissistic personality disorder, or a superiority complex. It is a manic defense against the possibility of separation and loss.

When megalomania is linked to a position of power, such as in Adolf Hitler or an Islamic dictator such as an "Ayatollah", there are normally disastrous consequences. This is because the megalomaniac who has political and military power if not complete control of its citizenry, is with this disorder, likely to miscalculate the communications and conduct of other nations.

---

100 <u>Is Germany Incurable?</u> by Richard Brickner, M.D., 1943, pp. 31-32

The <u>American College Dictionary</u> defines megalomania as "a form of mental alienation marked by delusions of greatness, wealth, etc.; a mania for big or great things."[101] Symptoms of megalomania were observed everywhere in Germany in the World War Two era. Here are two mentions of the disorder. The first quotation is in reference to a speech by Joseph Goebbels, whose official title under Hitler was Minister of Propaganda and Public Enlightenment:

"The words of prominent Nazi leaders are often quoted to illustrate the extreme limits to which 'Nazi' megalomania has gone. A famous example is the dictum of Goebbels at a Berlin mass meeting in March, 1936, that "there can be no opposition to National Socialism for the National Socialist is always right. Those who are not National Socialists can never be right. What right have they to criticize?" [102]

"Megalomania is unmistakable in the colossal Nazi pageantries, reeking with theatricalized, synthetic grandeur--blazing spotlights, insistent martial music, massed banners, cheering in unison, roaring loudspeakers--and the melodramatically timed entrance of the Fuhrer, symbol of the paranoid thirst for self-aggrandizement." [103]

Muslims exhibit the same tendencies, as they assemble and demonstrate in like manner with large mobs, to shout over and over the words "there is no god but Allah, and Mohammed is his prophet."

---

101 <u>American College Dictionary</u> by C.L. Barnhart, Editor, 1963, p. 757
102 <u>Is Germany Incurable?</u> by Richard Brickner, M.D., 1943, p. 171
103 <u>Is Germany Incurable?</u> by Richard Brickner, M.D., 1943, p. 268

Chants and banners of "death to the enemies of Allah" are heard and seen at the funeral processions for Islamic terrorists.

Militant Muslims are not averse to kidnapping and terror because they think very highly of themselves, which automatically lowers the value of others. Islamists in Iran held 66 American diplomats and others against their will, as hostages, ill kept and ill fed, at the U.S. embassy in Tehran, Iran, for 444 days in 1979-1981 during the presidency of Jimmy Carter. Appeasement never works with paranoids! The hostages were released within hours of successor Ronald Reagan's inauguration as President of the United States in January, 1981, because of Mr. Reagan's unequivocal statements that he would send a military force to deliver the American hostages from captivity as his first act of business following his swearing in to the office as President of the United States.

The combination of megalomania in the leadership of armed nations, coupled with paranoid tendencies, spells trouble for peace on the earth because Fascist behavior ensues. Appeasement is not possible. One author gave this definition of Fascist's behavior:

> *"Fascism is nothing but the primitive though somewhat disguised desire for power."* [104]

Violent aggression by Islamic peoples from many countries has resulted in a so-called "war on terror" by Western nations, which would be more accurately named "war on Islamic terror". But the effort is complicated by the fact that political correctness of our

---

104 <u>The Nazis Go Underground</u> by Curt Riess, 1944, p. 199

day prohibits the religion of Islam from being named as the culprit. Also, Islamic terrorists hail from dozens of Islamic-ruled nations, not just one or two countries. The terrorist attacks, such as at the Boston Marathon in 2013 are known to be carried out by Muslims, yet the "religion" of Islam, which spawns such attacks avoids prosecution.

"For, when pushed too far, in justice to his outraged majesty, in cold rage at the world's diabolically malevolent thwarting, the paranoid kills, committing not a sudden crime of passion, but deliberate, well-executed, self-righteous murder." [105]

The description of violence above, fits perfectly the behavior seen in Nazi Germany in an earlier day, and today's followers of Mohammed. Islam is a Fascist, political cause, not a religion! Muslims paraded and danced in the streets of many Mid-Eastern Islamic nations when more than 3,000 innocents perished in the well planned attacks in New York, Washington and Pennsylvania in addition to literally billions of dollars of property damage in the Islamic terrorist attacks of September 11, 2001. If hate is a religion, then and only then is Islam a religion.

---

105 Is Germany Incurable? by Richard Brickner, M.D., 1943, p. 32

CHAPTER 5

Fascists intolerance
of all other dogmas

———

THE KORAN, SUPPOSEDLY WRITTEN BY a violent man named
Mohammed, purports to be the way to follow the mythical god
of Islam, Allah. Intolerant of any other beliefs, the Koran dictates Fascist violence and death to the adversaries of Islam. It also
preaches the superiority of Islam to the blind drones who are mandated to follow this fruitless religion.

The Koran urges its followers to "strike terror into the hearts
of the enemies of Allah" (Koran 8:60) and to fight and die for
Islam:

*"Indeed, Allah has purchased from the believers their lives
and their properties; for that they will have Paradise. They
fight in the cause of Allah, so they kill and are killed.(Koran
9:111)"* [106]

---

106 The Complete Infidel's Guide to ISIS by Robert Spencer, p.21

The Muslim "holy book" the Koran says behead your enemies:

"When you meet the unbelievers, strike the necks" (Koran 47:4) [107]

This intolerance parallels Fascist Nazism. In the Hitler-penned book Mein Kampf, or "my battle," Hitler gave his design or outline of what a future Germany would be like as lord of the whole earth. A distinct view of life is described with Germans as masters and everyone else as servants. One commentary on Hitler's book noted:

"That this view of life would strike a normal mind of the twentieth century as a grotesque hodgepodge concocted by a half-baked, uneducated neurotic goes without saying. What makes it important is that it was embraced so fanatically by so many millions of Germans and that if it led, as it did, to their ultimate ruin it also led to the ruin of so many millions of innocent, decent human beings inside and especially outside Germany." [108]

In the Hitler reign of Germany (1933-1945), the attitude and atmosphere of Germany toward war had been carefully and successfully developed for decades by many German philosophers and social scientists:

"...radical reactionaries like Ruppert who presented war as the 'fulfillment of human existence,' and Banse who saw in war the 'everlasting yea of the active warlike man.'" [109]

---

107 Ibid., p.226
108 The Rise and Fall of the Third Reich, by William L.Shirer, 1960, p. 82
109 German Psychological Warfare by Ladislas Farago, 1942, p. 6

A 1930 publication in Berlin by Junker and Duennhaupt was entitled <u>The Moral Justification of War and Idea of Permanent Peace,</u> in summation:

> *"...justifies war as a necessary phenomenon in the nationalist tradition. He agrees with Moltke that permanent peace is a dream--and not a pretty one at that. Only a nation that has preserved its will to wage war deserves to continue its existence.*[110]

Haushofer's 1932 book on military geopolitics brought forth the concept of the need for German "living space," defined as foreign lands designated by political leaders as desirable and then acquired by Germany through military force:

> *"He was Hitler's greatest influence in the writing of Mein Kampf and is primarily known as the inventor of the Nazi slogan--'living space.'"*[111]

Because Fascists have no tolerance for any other dogma, Germany's thirty million Catholics were targeted by Hitler, as enemies of the Reich. In June, 1934, just 18 months after Hitler came to power, Hitler declared the Catholic Youth Movement illegal, and named them as "traitors to the German people."[112] All the Catholic leaders of the Catholic Youth Movement group were arrested, tortured and imprisoned indefinitely. Many were executed. The Nazis called the Catholics "black swine."[113]

---

110 Ibid., p. 184
111 Ibid., p. 186
112 <u>Four Years of Nazi Torture</u> by Ernst Winkler, 1943, p. 2
113 <u>Ibid.,</u> p. 4

Since the Catholic religion was headquartered in Rome, Hitler deemed Catholicism as disloyal and sinister to his own German fatherland causes:

In the early weeks of July, 1941, the great Catholic areas of the Rhineland, Bavaria, Westphalia, former Austria, and Sudetenland among others found themselves in the throes of a new Nazi wave of oppression, featured chiefly by the wholesale closing down of convents and cloisters. Uniformed men of the S.S. and non-uniformed men of the Gestapo swarmed into towns and villages, rudely dispossessing nuns and priests alike and driving them into the streets without notice.[114]

Catholic convents and other buildings were taken over and turned into dormitories for Germans brought back from other countries. Priests and large supporters of Catholic churches were subjected to telephone calls at all hours of the night, and threatening letters from the Nazi hierarchy. Nazi S.S. troops attended Mass to listen for anything that might be said by priests which could indict them for crimes of treason against the State.

MILITANT ISLAM MIRRORS NAZI FASCISM

First, the followers of Fascist Islam relinquish personal rights and freedoms to an all-powerful State in the form of an all-powerful religion. Then, they become hurtful to many outsiders elsewhere on the planet by the beliefs inculcated. As it was with Nazi Germany, so it is with militant, Fascist Islam today.

---

114 The Foe We Face by Pierre Huss, 1942, p. 236

In 2015, a mass exodus of refugees have fled into Europe from the Mideast because of Muslim sectarian violence. They are not migrants! Hundreds of thousands of refugees headed, not for other Muslim countries, but for the safety that is inherent in non-Muslim countries where law and order and a stable society are the rule, not the exception. Militant Muslims are also camouflaged among these refugees.

Can anyone picture a natural disaster or pestilence of some sort which would mandate a flow of hundreds of thousands of Christians or Catholics INTO the Muslim-dominated Mideast? That could not happen. The Muslim community of nations there such as Iraq, Iran, Saudi Arabia and Pakistan would not tolerate such an inflow of non-Muslims. Yet the non-Muslim western nations are automatically assumed to not only tolerate, but to instantly welcome the permanent relocation of hundreds of thousands of people, most of them Muslims.

Twenty-two militant Islamic nations have formed an organization called the "Arab League." The Muslim population of these 22 nations is more than 334 million people.[115] These nations have sufficient military might to snuff out the ISIS terrorist group that is plaguing Syria and parts of Iraq. But they are not doing that. Why would they not care about preserving the homes and lands of their Muslim brothers? Perhaps it is part of the plan to spread Islamic control faster throughout western Europe by emigration. Why aren't the people fleeing to nearby, super-rich Saudi Arabia? Because they are not welcome there!

---

115 https://en.wikipedia.org/wiki/Islam_by_country

Violence is the calling card of Fascism. Is the intended spread of Islam bringing more peace, freedom and tranquility to any countries of the world? No, quite the opposite. Nations which are governed by Islamic Sharia law are in the main, backward, uncivilized, unstable, and un-hospitable to all neighbors. Personal freedoms such as freedom of speech and religion are nonexistent, and women are regarded as slaves (or worse) with few or no rights.

Often, Muslim acts of terrorism are executed simply because of supposed outrage on the part of Muslims for what non-Muslims say or do in regard to Islam. That outrage against free speech or closely held opinions justifies the violence that Muslims carry out--in the view of the offended Muslim(s).

But, one might say, why is Fascism tantamount to violent action? Because Fascists demand and then take by force what does not belong to them. Consider Hitler's discourse in his book <u>Mein Kampf</u>, about taking what belongs to others. All the land of western Europe was taken by force and occupied in Hitler's time. A quote from Hitler's own book (Mein Kampf) as recounted by William Shirer:

> *"but nature has not reserved this soil for the future possession of any particular nation or race; on the contrary, this soil exists for the people which possesses the force to take it."* [116]

---

116 <u>The Rise and Fall of the Third Reich</u>, by William L.Shirer, 1960, p. 82

Fascist systems seize what does not belong to them by force, unless fought against and stopped. Very naturally, Fascists become the scourge of a freedom loving world:

> *"The aggressions against Denmark, Norway, Holland, Belgium and Luxembourg afford further proof, if necessary, that in the exercise of the right of the stronger, Hitlerite Germany, unrestrained by respect for the pledged word and the law, openly flouts the indignation and contempt of all civilized peoples."* [117]

The Fascist ideology of Islam desires that the entire world be under its thumb as to how to live, and by whom every facet of life is to be governed. There is no question about the goal of Islam. Extreme violence, terror and intimidation are its modus operandi to bring about the subjection of more people groups and entire nations not already afflicted with this monstrous disease.

---

117 I Paid Hitler by Fritz Thyssen, 1941, p. 283

CHAPTER 6

Fascist hatred drives rule by terror

———

MAKE NO MISTAKE ABOUT IT, hate is a religion. One can try to reason with its adherents or make treaties with such as are driven by hate, but such measures are in vain if the hater also has power to injure others.

HATRED PERFECTED--NAZI TERROR

By targeting certain groups for hatred, discrimination, violence or death, fascists elevate themselves above those they deem inferior or unworthy of life itself. Hatred is destructive to the hater and the hated. Hate, when coupled with paranoia and a high opinion of oneself, brings dangerous machinations. Under Hitler's Fascism, Germany persecuted, disenfranchised, imprisoned, starved or murdered its enemies outright or by subtlety. The enemies were Jews, Christians, labor unions, mental patients, Freemasons, Poles, Negroes, Slavs, and many others.

The worst outcome was to German Jews in loss of property, in freedoms and eventually of their lives. One estimate of Nazi theft is that they took $7 billion in property, goods, and money from German Jews alone, including the proceeds of auctions of stolen goods.[118]

Within two weeks of the German armies marching into Austria to take over that country in 1938, Jewish people were hurled into catastrophe. Homes and businesses of Jews were looted and taken over. Hitler directed his hordes of soldiers to humiliate and diminish Jewish people as one eyewitness describes in Vienna, on March 22, 1938:

"On the street today gangs of Jews, with jeering storm troopers standing over them and taunting crowds around them, on their hands and knees scrubbing the Schuschnigg signs off the sidewalks. Many Jews killing themselves. All sorts of reports of Nazi sadism, and from the Austrians it surprises me. Jewish men and women made to clean latrines. Hundreds of them just picked at random off the streets to clean the toilets of the Nazi boys."[119]

"Adolf Hitler had at last arrived; but he was not alone. He had called from the depths of defeat the dark and savage furies latent in the most numerous, most serviceable, ruthless, contradictory, and ill-starred race in Europe. He had conjured up the fearful idol of an all-devouring Moloch of which he

---

118 <u>This Is The Enemy</u> by Frederick Oechsner, 1942, p. 310
119 <u>Berlin Diary</u> by William Shirer, 1941, pp. 110-111

was the priest and incarnation. It is not within my scope to describe the inconceivable brutality and villainy by which this apparatus of hatred and tyranny had been fashioned and was now to be perfected." [120]

To Adolf Hitler, both the Jews and the Slavic people were called the "Untermenschen" or sub-humans. He stated they had no right to live, except as slaves in fields and mines. Their culture was to be stamped out and formal education denied to them.[121]

German dictator Adolf Hitler next demanded that the Sudetenland, part of Czechoslovakia, be returned to Germany. This demand was granted by the major powers of France and England, though it was not theirs to give! The country of Czechoslovakia became a pawn in a deadly game. While demanding the Sudetenland, Hitler actually sent troops in and also took the entire provinces of Bohemia and Moravia on March 15, 1939, and declared the balance of Czechoslovakia a "German protectorate."

Czechs had to flee these areas, as Germans were sent in to take possession of houses, lands and businesses which they neither bought nor paid for. The following day, all firearms were ordered to be turned in to the occupying government, with the penalty of death for possession of any guns after a brief period. Thorough, impromptu house searches were made repeatedly by the German Gestapo to root out any who would dare to possess a firearm. This made future resistance against tyranny impossible.

---

120 <u>The Gathering Storm</u> by Winston Churchill, 1948, pp. 70-71
121 <u>The Rise and Fall of the Third Reich</u> by William Shirer, 1960, p.937

With the additional losses to Czechoslovakia of southern Slovakia by neighboring Hungarian annexation, and annexation of part of Silesia by Poland, the Czech nation lost 1,200,000 people, or one quarter of the nations population, to foreign rule. Weak political leadership in both Czechoslovakia and the western powers brought this about through appeasement toward Hitler.[122] (We must remember that megalomaniacs cannot be appeased, and the demands never cease.)

The rape and pillaging of Czechoslovakia continued quickly under Hitler's Fascism. Beginning April 5, 1939, less than three weeks after the takeover of the country, Nazi overseers (called Treuhanders) were placed in every business to oversee them, giving the Nazis firm control of the economy.[123]

Fascists aspire to control the speech and even the thoughts of their subjects. We see this evidenced in Czechoslovakia, where during that country's six year domination by Germany, the press was controlled by the Nazis, and rules laid down about trying to gather news from other outside sources:

"Fortunately, our radio happened to be out of order. The Gestapo would often set a household's radio dial on the London frequency and execute the entire family for listening to London." [124]

It got worse yet under German Fascism. Martial law was declared in Czechoslavakia, eliminating all personal freedoms and

---

122 <u>Tomorrow Will Be Better</u> by Zdena Kapral, 1990, pp. 45-49
123 Ibid., p. 61
124 Ibid., p. 140

requiring every person who might travel to another village or city by walking or any other conveyance, to immediately register with the local police upon entering the place. Naturally, the purpose of such a visit away from one's own domicile had to be legitimate in the eyes of the German police, or trouble followed.

Mass murder was carried out by Nazi Fascists all during the Second World War. Sometimes it was in retaliation for the killing of a German soldier, usually ten citizens of the occupied country were chosen at random and shot or hung for each German soldier killed. It was many more than that at times. When Nazi ruler Heydrich was murdered in Czechoslovakia, Hitler ordered the murder of 80-120 Czech citizens per day until the murderers of Heydrich were surrendered to the Nazis.[125]

THE GUILLOTINE

Strange as it may seem, executing one's enemies by chopping off their heads has great appeal to Fascists. Political prisoners in Czechoslovakia were kept by the sadistic Nazis in a prison in Breslau. Many men were arrested, kept there, beaten repeatedly and then murdered without ever having been charged with a crime. But every Thursday at Breslau, 50-100 Czechs were beheaded by guillotine.[126] Fascists are a law unto themselves, and owe no one an explanation for their conduct. (The Muslims of our day also portend to answer to no one for what they do.)

---

125 <u>Tomorrow Will Be Better</u> by Zdena Kapral, 1990, p. 98
126 Ibid., p. 221

OTHER ACTS OF EXTREME VIOLENCE MARK NAZI FASCISM

The hatred and targeting of certain groups of people for the harshest treatment by Fascists is apparent, though irrational. For example, the Nazis blamed Jewish bankers for Germany's shattered economy in the years following the First World War. But the Jewish bankers had actually saved the German economy, thanks to Jews who obtained loans for many small and medium sized companies from American banks and investment houses such as Goldman Sachs. None of these Jewish banks survived with Hitler in power.[127]

On April 6, 1941, Hitler's forces bombed the city of Belgrade, Yugoslavia, in a brazen, premeditated attack on the country designed to cause the country to surrender and yield to Nazi Germany rule. The dead were piled everywhere in the downtown area. A journalist wrote of it:

"What I wanted to find out was what had killed these people. The one I examined didn't have a single wound you could see. They had probably all been killed just by the repercussion that knocked them down, like ninepins, and did a swift, merciful bloodless job of it. I kept thinking it was too bad that everyone hadn't been killed that way. It was clean.

I told you that all the bodies lay in the doorways. That isn't exactly true. There was one body on the sidewalk. I couldn't help stopping to look at it. She lay on her side. She had on a sky-blue shimmery evening dress. Her hair was rich brown and perfectly combed. I looked down at her and wondered

---

127 <u>I Paid Hitler</u> by Fritz Thyssen, 1941, p. 218-219

*where she had been last night, to still have on an evening dress
at five o'clock in the morning. The gown had slipped down
off her right shoulder. It was the kind of a shoulder a sculptor
would have chiseled. Then I noticed her right leg. Half of it
was gone."* [128]

The same treatment was in store for every country that became occupied and enslaved by Nazi Germany. A Polish man was caught
by the Gestapo trying to reach French soil to join other Poles in
fighting with the Allies against Germany. He recalled one of the
many torture sessions with four Gestapo men who wanted the
names and location of any and all compatriots:

*"He nodded to the men behind me and clasped his hands on
his stomach. This was the signal for one of the men to rap me
sharply behind the ear with the rubber stick. A vivid, agonizing
pain shot through my entire body as if a bolt of lightning had
gone through me. Of all the beatings I have endured, I never
felt anything to equal the instant of sheer pain produced by the
impact of the rubber truncheon. It made every muscle in my
body wince in sharp agony. It was something like the sensation
produced when a dentist's drill strikes a nerve, but infinitely
multiplied and spread over the entire nervous system."* [129]

Consider the Nazi takeover of Paris in World War Two. As German
troops approached Paris in June, 1940, two million unarmed civilians fled via automobile, truck, horse cart, or on foot.[130] Thousands

128 <u>From the Land of Silent People</u> by Robert St. John, 1943, p. 61
129 <u>Story of A Secret State</u> by Jan Karski 1944, p. 152
130 <u>Liberation</u> by Martin Blumenson, 1978, p. 118

of them were murdered by Nazi fighter planes as the refugees were stranded in an endless traffic jam fleeing the city of Paris. Worse yet, it was a planned massacre.

"The hum became a roar, as the airplane passed by just ahead of us, and from the roar emerged the staccato tat-tat-tat of a machine gun. We could see the hulk of the plane in a denser black against the dark sky, and the flame spitting from the nozzles of its guns, as it swept over the crowded road, pouring death into the trapped ranks below. In a matter of seconds, the crowded highway was emptied of its human freight. Terror-stricken drivers turned their cars off the road, into trees, into ditches, over the fields. Some of them overturned, and their occupants squirmed out and ran in panic from the road, or threw themselves into ditches. Only a few cars remained in the road, stalled, motionless. The figures in them were motionless, too. They had not joined the mad rush to get off the road because they were dead. They had been mowed down indiscriminately, men, women and children, by the sudden hail of death that had rained down upon them out of the sky." [131]

The panic and subsequent violence for Paris and other French cities was all carefully planned by Nazi Germany, as they warred against France. Fake phone calls were made to mayors of many cities, claiming high French military authority, with warnings given that their towns were going to be bombed by the enemy. The mayors were ordered to evacuate the townspeople. Then the retreating Frenchmen were machine-gunned from Nazi fighter planes flying

---

131 <u>Paris Underground</u> by Etta Shiber 1943, p. 22

overhead as they fled on roadways, where no military targets what-soever were present. This is mass murder, typical of Fascists.

The Nazi Fascist aggression followed the same pattern every-where. In the spring takeover of Denmark for its alleged protection, Germany showed an unusual way to display its caring oversight. An unannounced, massive bombing raid of Copenhagen, Denmark resulted in the deaths of over 60,000 civilians and the total de-struction of 28,000 buildings.

Tactics of free nations in conducting war are markedly different, if at all possible. American tactics in World War Two were different in the first place because the war against Germany was a declared war. America and its Allies sought the destruction of Germany's ability to make war. Even so, General Dwight Eisenhower tried to warn German citizens of impending heavy Allied bombing in their homeland. As the war escalated on German soil, pamphlets bear-ing Eisenhower's name and personal signature were dropped in and around large cities such as Frankfurt and Mannheim, warning the residents expressly that their cities:

> *"...from now on will be subjected to merciless bombardment...*
> *no shelter or refuge within the above named districts can be*
> *considered safe. Every inhabitant...is hereby warned to remove*
> *himself and his family immediately to a safe place outside the*
> *battle area."* [132]

Contrariwise, mass terror murder of unarmed civilians was a trait common to Hitler's Germany and is common to present

---

132 <u>Paper Bullets</u> by Leo Margolin, 1946, p. 63

day Islam. Islamic terrorists kill even young schoolchildren in great numbers without remorse. This is reminiscent of Himmler's SS Death Squads (Einsatzgruppen) which followed German armies as they advanced into Russia. In the area of Riga, Russia, alone, captured post-war Nazi records showed that by October, 1941, just four months after Germany's invasion of Russia, 58,000 Jews had been summarily shot and killed by the Death Squads.[133]

> *"Their task was the systematic murder of people for whom there was no place in the Nazi state. These would include the commissars (political officers attached to Red Army units), guerrillas, saboteurs, Jews and Bolshevik agitators. In practice, the Einsatzgruppen sought out and killed not only Jews but all educated people, especially those who were socially influential, such as doctors, teachers, writers, priests and rabbis. Their families were not exempt. During the remaining months of 1941 about 500,000 European Russian Jews were slaughtered by these teams, and perhaps as many non-Jewish Russians as well."* [134]

A naive world goes about life making heroes of terrorists, whether they be charismatic fast talkers like Adolf Hitler, scientists like the father of modern rocketry, Werner Von Braun, or a Muslim terrorist brandishing an AK-47 rifle. But truth imparts wisdom. For example, when Werner Von Braun, the inventor of the Nazi V-2 rocket bomb which killed and maimed thousands of unarmed

---

133 <u>The Foe We Face</u> by Pierre Huss, 1942, p. 246
134 <u>Blood, Tears and Folly</u> by Len Deighton, 1993, p. 473

British citizens, was arrested after Victory in Europe, he expressed disappointment that the Germans had not been able to use the V-2 rocket for a longer time.[135]

Martin Bormann, an important Nazi party deputy under Hitler, worked for the elimination of Nazi Germany's supposed enemies. He made this statement about them in 1938:

"I for one shall never rest until the last Jew is gone and until all the churches in Germany serve the Fatherland and God instead of some outside power. A lot of us feel the same way... Well, then, what else is the Vatican but a foreign power telling some 30 million Germans how to act and to be loyal first and foremost to the Vatican."[136]

Bormann also conducted the terror campaign against the Jews in Germany. Whether it was telephone calls in the night from the Gestapo, or the sudden arrest of a Jewish family next door:

"Jews came around to us with blanched faces, in the depths of despair, fully cognizant by now of the sworn oaths of Bormann that before the end of 1941 not a single Jew would be left inside Germany. The lid was off; Bormann was riding high and the Gestapo and S.S. pounced like packs of hungry wolves on the Jews."[137]

---

135 <u>This Must Not Happen Again! The Black Book of Fascist Horror</u> by Clark Kinnaird, 1945, p. 78
136 <u>The Foe We Face</u> by Pierre Huss, 1942, p. 230
137 Ibid., p. 249-250

The Gestapo and S.S. troops would knock on the doors of Jewish homes and apartments after 11 p.m., giving the residents one hour to be ready to leave with no more than 30 pounds of clothes and other possessions in hand. Loaded in trucks, thousands of Jews were shipped to death camps in Poland and elsewhere. Meanwhile, their homes were sealed by order of the Secret Police until auctions were scheduled, to sell all furniture and other possessions and the premises occupied by Nazi party members or German soldiers. In Berlin alone, 86,000 Jews had been taken away to their deaths in Poland from January to November, 1941.[138]

As we know from history, the Nazis murdered six million Jews in Europe in World War Two. Their treachery in deporting Jews from their homes in the city of Paris, France, to their death, reminds one of the deadly, sneak attacks Islam employs. Here is one description of Nazi German treachery in deportations:

"The stereotype of the Jew as crafty, cunning and unscrupulous was totally contradicted in practice when roughly 70,000 Jews meekly let themselves be arrested, deported, and gassed, thanks to the use of obvious tricks and transparent lies. How easy it was to encourage them with false hopes at the point of departure by telling them they needed work boots and giving them a few zlotys (Polish currency), how easy to fool them at the end of the journey with bath towels and dummy shower heads. The Jews were ingenuous. They believed what they were told." [139]

---

138 Ibid., p. 252
139 <u>An Uncertain Hour</u> by Ted Morgan 1990, p. 193

"Many soldiers and American civilians have already forgotten the mountains of shoes of all sizes, from baby size to the largest adult size, which our troops uncovered in German murder camp after murder camp. The thing which amazes psychological warfare experts is the naivete of Americans, military and civilian, whose memories are so short they forget that Germany declared war on the United States (December 11, 1941), not the other way around. And that hundreds of American soldiers taken prisoner were treated not unlike the millions of innocent European civilians, deliberately starved and then slaughtered by the Germans between 1933 and 1945." [140]

The most diabolical of all Nazi heinous tactics was the black bordered death card sent by the regular mail to hundreds of Jews in the city of Berlin. Many Jews committed suicide when they received this notice. Printed in black typeface with palm branches at the bottom, the notice read as follows:

"You are instructed herewith to deliver your useless person at 3 p.m. tomorrow to the ground back of Lichtenberg cemetery, equipped with spade or shovel, to dig the hole in which you will lie with other Jews after liquidation of your carcass free of cost." [141]

Certainly America had racial prejudice in its history, with the slavery of blacks. The Civil War of course did not end the controversy. It took nearly a century after the Civil War for Americans, especially in the south, to stop segregating blacks from whites,

---

140 <u>Paper Bullets</u> by Leo Margolin 1946, p. 136
141 <u>The Foe We Face</u> by Pierre Huss, 1942, p. 248-249

and to strive for racial equality. Yet true racism under Hitler was not to be compared.

In World War Two, the American military had not yet been racially integrated. This happened under President Truman after the war. There were many widely acclaimed black combat units, fighter squadrons of black pilots, and other elements of American military in World War Two!

A black soldier named Sergeant Leon Bass fought for his native America in the war, and thought he knew racial discrimination and hatred, until he saw what was done to the racial enemies of Nazis at a death camp inside Germany:

> *"I came into that camp (Buchenwald) an angry black soldier. Angry at my country and justifiably so. Angry because they were treating me as though I was not good enough. But that day I came to the realization that human suffering is not relegated to me and mine. I now knew that human suffering could touch us all...What I saw in Buchenwald was the face of evil...it was racism."* [142]

It was no longer a secret in Germany that Jews were imperiled. The nightmare for Jews had begun, just a few months after Hitler came to power in 1933:

> *"The first essential step was to prepare the public mind and arouse antagonism against every Jew. I remember well the days of late summer in Berlin, when propaganda slogans from*

---

142 <u>Liberators</u> by Lou Potter, 1992, p. 207

all sides shrieked suddenly that the Jew was the enemy of all Germany...They had suddenly been ordered to give up room apartments or move on short notice into crowded quarters assigned to them with other Jewish families." [143]

It was no secret, yet all the citizenry of Germany by and large feared a concentration or labor camp for themselves to such an extent that there was virtually no organized opposition to the holocaust, the slaughter of the Jews by Hitler's Germany. A word spoken against the Nazi party or its leaders was tantamount to a beating, prison, or a death camp.

The liquidation of Jews was well known to grown-ups in Germany during World War Two. Frequent, brazen articles appeared in German newspapers, such as the one by Nazi Kurt Kraenzlein, in the fall of 1941 which openly called for the final liquidation of Jews on the European continent.

In neighboring Romania, guns were firing away at Jews in full cooperation with the Nazis directive there in 1941. In the city of Nikolayev, 4,000 Jews were killed in one day. In Otchav, Romania, a fourteen year old boy was observed shooting a gun, and was asked what he was shooting at. His reply:

" 'Jews,' the Romanian lad replied. 'I get five lei for every one I kill. On this stick in my hand I have thirty-four notches, each made by a policeman I show the dead Jew to. When I have fifty, then I get an extra bonus. It is only three o'clock in the afternoon and it will not be dark for three hours. I may get the fifty.' " [144]

---

143 <u>The Foe We Face</u> by Pierre Huss, 1942, p. 243-244
144 Ibid., p. 247

The principal goal of Hitler's Germany was world rule in World War Two, by getting rid of all opposition:

"From the beginning, theft of property and literal enslavement of large numbers of persons of all religious faiths was carried on in Germany under guise of laws for protection of the state. The Germans made no distinctions in conquered countries, either. In Holland, a typical example, 940,000 persons--10% of Holland's population, were deprived of their property and sent to concentration or extermination camps. Only 140,000 of these were Jews." [145]

The violence against those deemed undesirable or hated in Nazi Germany, included its own citizenry indeed, constantly under threat of reprisals for opposition to or disagreement with the actions of the dictator Adolf Hitler:

"There were also detention camps and carefully broadcast hints of what might be in store for anyone who had temerity enough to inquire into his methods too closely, let alone openly disapprove of them." [146]

"Dateline Berlin, Germany, November 18, 1939--"Here in Germany three youths were executed yesterday for 'treason.' And two youngsters aged nineteen were sentenced to death in Augsburg today for having committed theft in the home of a soldier." [147]

---

145 <u>This Must Not Happen Again! The Black Book of Fascist Horror</u> by Clark Kinnaird, 1945, p. 23

146 <u>The Past is Myself</u> by Christabel Bielenberg, 1972, p. 28

147 <u>Berlin Diary</u> by William Schirer, 1941, p. 249

The citizenry of Germany knew only too well that their civil rights were nonexistent under Hitler's Fascism. News articles gave people a clear picture. Total war was the decree, and industrial production was tilted heavily toward the mining, refining and production of war materials in Germany and in Nazi-occupied countries. Nothing stood in the way of making arms, and the newspapers carried stories to get the point across to the citizenry:

> *"Berlin, October 31, 1939: The secret police announced that two men were shot for 'resisting arrest' yesterday. One of them, it is stated, was trying to induce some German workers to lay down their tools in an important armament factory. Himmler now has power to shoot anyone he likes without trial."* [148]

FASCIST TERROR TODAY

A learned Muslim scholar and teacher named Dr. Khalid Duran has been speaking out against radical Islam for many years. Born in Spain, educated in Pakistan and Germany, Duran has traveled over the length and breadth of Islam in the Mideast. This is what he said about the Muslim Brotherhood, an organization which joins other radical Islamic groups in terrorism, working together toward building an Islamic world:

> *"People don't remember, but the Muslim Brotherhood grew up in Egypt in the 1930's as an imitation of European Fascism, which was also a revolt against modernity. In Italy and Germany you had the brownshirts and the blackshirts.*

---

148 <u>Berlin Diary</u> by William Schirer, 1941, p. 241.

*In Egypt you had the greenshirts, which was the Muslim
Brotherhood. It failed in Europe but survived in Egypt and
spread to other parts of the Islamic world."* [149]

Yes, Islam is Fascism! Hate-inspired violence is the calling card of
any Fascist ideology. Islamic terrorists are at work around the world
bombing, threatening, carrying out subterfuge against Islamic and
non-Islamic peoples, and summarily executing its enemies, usually by decapitation. This violence is intended to intimidate non-
Islamic nations, so that they eventually give in and surrender to the
demands and the laws of Islam.

Muslims emigrate to non-Islamic countries in order to take
a country over through peaceful means by proselytizing, bearing
large families, fomenting racial unrest and discontent with the
government, and by initiating guerrilla warfare. The Nazi Fascists
had their own tactics for diminishing opposition to their criminal
terrorist rule, such as the pronouncements of Heinrich Himmler,
head of the German State Secret Police, otherwise known as the
Gestapo or SS Forces:

*"The S. S. Fuehrer saw more clearly than the Minister that the
purpose of the concentration camps was not only to punish enemies of the regime but by their very existence to terrorize the
people and deter them from even contemplating any resistance
to Nazi rule."* [150]

---

149 American Jihad: The Terrorists Living Among Us by Steven Emerson, 2002,
p. 172
150 The Rise and Fall of the Third Reich, by William L.Shirer, 1960, p. 271

HATRED PERFECTED--ISLAMIC TERROR

Who could deny that militant Islam is dedicated to putting their fear into the masses? Islamic nations punish their own citizens for crimes real or perceived, such as the May, 2014 news story of a pregnant Sudanese Christian woman scheduled to be beaten, then executed for having married a Christian man. Islam does not recognize Christian marriage! And publishing such punishments helps keeps Islamic automaton populations in line.

Islamic militants have and are committing atrocities daily in the world, such as the ghastly murders of nearly 60 innocent, young boys in a Christian school in Nigeria, Africa in April, 2014. All were shot outright in their dormitory. In the same month, the kidnapping of 300 teenage girls from a Christian school, also in Nigeria, Africa, with the intent of selling the females into Islamic sexual slavery. In December, 2014, over 140 young boys were shot to death by Islamic terrorists in a school in Pakistan. Is not Islam the enemy of all freedom and righteousness? Who will stop this naked Fascist violence carried out in the name of religion?

In the world today, Muslims the world over cry out "Death to Israel" and "Death to America." Why? That is simply the Fascist agenda--war, murder, extermination, and domination! Muslims kill schoolchildren by the score, or other innocents. Thirty-seven tourists were murdered in Ondon, Tunisia on the shore of the Mediterranean Sea and in neighboring hotels by Islamic terrorists on June 26, 2015, according to Cable News Network. This was an attempt to scare people away from the area with the threat of violence, to hurt the economy of that region. This type of planned violent attack occurs with regularity somewhere on the earth.

On June 28, 2015, for example, a man was beheaded by a Muslim in Lyons, France at a large, American owned gas utility plant. Fox news reported:

"Despite mimicking the practices of Islamic extremists, no foreign group has claimed responsibility for the attack. The attack also came days after the Islamic State urged attacks during the Muslim holy month of Ramadan." [151]

If murderous attacks by Muslims are urged during a supposed holy time, then Islam is indeed a religion of hate. The pattern of extreme Fascist behavior in Islam continues on every continent in the world today without interruption. How long will this "religion" be tolerated by free men?

It was July 16, 2015, when a Kuwait-born Muslim opened fire in two U.S. Navy recruitment offices in the Chattanooga, Tennessee area, killing four unarmed U.S. Marines and a U.S. Navy sailor before being shot to death by police.[152] Does this shock anyone that Mohammedans are at war with anyone and everyone who is not Muslim?

The violence continues apace, as on December 2, 2015 in San Bernadino, California a "lone wolf" Muslim terrorist attack by a Muslim man and his wife murdered fourteen people by gunfire and injured scores of others, having sworn allegiance to the cause of Islamic jihad. The couple was shot and killed by police in a gun battle shortly thereafter.

---

151 Foxnews.com/world news, June 28, 2015
152 Foxnews.com/world news, July 17, 2015

CHAPTER 7

Preparation for continual warfare

———

UNDER HITLER AS WELL AS under Kaiser Wilhelm II, attitudes were shaped fostering international anti-Communism, anti-Semitism and anti-capitalism all in the same breath. Anything contrary to the State religion (Fascism) was to be forever fought and eliminated. Howard K. Smith, a well known American journalist and television news broadcaster, lived in Germany for over five years, and saw Germany transformed by design into a Fascist empire. He wrote:

> *"The Germany-at-war to which I returned was little different from the Germany-at-peace I had left. In a state created expressly for the purpose of waging war, the line dividing the two conditions was bound to be a fine, almost invisible one."* [153]

The climate of militarism grew quickly after Adolf Hitler's 1933 ascension to power as the Supreme leader (Chancellor) of the State of Germany. Hitler repeatedly violated the Treaty of Versailles,

———

153 <u>Last Train From Berlin</u> by Howard K. Smith 1942, p. 52

which ended World War One, by a build-up of military forces and machinery for war. It was well planned by Hitler for the so called "greater good of Germany." News correspondent Howard K. Smith saw it in the entire warp and woof of German life:

> *"You began to grasp that what was happening was that young humans, millions of them, were being trained to act merely upon reflexes. And you inevitably came to wonder, what, after all, is the ultimate, the final reflex toward which all this drilling is directed? Obviously, to kill, as a reflex. To destroy 'according to plan'. On terse commands which altered their personalities more neatly than Doctor Jekyll became Mr. Hyde, they were learning to smash, crush, destroy, wreck.[154]*

Here is the dichotomy of good and evil, as expressed again by Howard K. Smith:

> *"A whole nation, for instance, which is unified as to means, methods, and an intense desire to abolish poverty and create abundance for all, could make the grandest civilization we have ever known, in a single generation. By the same token, a whole great nation which is unified in means, methods and will to carry out the single purpose of waging war could, if its neighbors were not equally determined, flood the world with blood and misery unequalled. That last is what I saw in Germany. I saw it before a month was out."[155]*

---

154 Ibid., p.13
155 <u>Last Train From Berlin</u> by Howard K. Smith 1942, p.16

Ciano, the son-in-law of Italy's fascist dictator Benito Mussolini, met with Hitler's Foreign Secretary Ribbentrop personally on August 11, 1939. At this juncture in history, Mussolini was trying to avoid widespread war, because of Italy's lack of military preparedness, and because an attack by Germany against Poland seemed imminent. Ciano's diary of this meeting records the Nazi's attitudes, and his descriptions from it brief and to the point, as reported back to his father-in-law:

> *"He has lied too many times about German intentions towards Poland not to feel uneasy now about what he must tell me, and what they are really planning to do. . .The German decision to fight is implacable. Even if they were given more than they ask, they would attack just the same, because they are possessed by the demon of destruction. . ."* [156]

Muslims are hailed to worldwide "jihad" or "holy war" against the enemies of Islam, which includes everyone and every country that is not headed up by a radical Islamic dictator and where all other religions are not banned. This has been the case for centuries, and is not simply a modern trend! For example, in a United States War Department review of the world military situation after World War Two, a simple description was given of the 90 million Muslims and the 300 million Hindus then living in India:

> *"The Moslems are warlike; Hindus are largely pacificists."* [157]

---

156 <u>The Gathering Storm</u> by Winston Churchill, 1948, p. 389

157 <u>Coast Artillery Journal,</u> Journal of the United States Army Artillery, May-June, 1946, p. 63

Hitler conditioned Germany for total war, which he brought about. Total war is described as "the collective effort of a coordinated nation to impose its will on other nations."[158] Do we not see a number of militant Muslim nations trying to impose their rule, religion and lifestyle on other nations right now? Muslim Shia and Sunni sects are at war with each other as well.

Tiny Israel, attacked constantly by Muslims, is surrounded by more than 20 radical, militant, Islamic dictatorships. The idea of a Muslim "holy war" is not new! Consider the article in the German newspaper <u>The Dresdener Zeitung</u>, of Monday, August 7, 1944, in which Heinrich Himmler, head of the Gestapo, talked of "holy people's war."[159] Yet Islam is a more insidious enemy than one identifiable enemy such as Germany under Kaiser Wilhelm II or Adolf Hitler.

Why is it that Fascists must promote continual warfare? It is expressly because Fascism is a violent ideology that is built on and run on the engine of aggression and hatred with the intent of gaining absolute control:

> *"Aggression, war-making propaganda at home and the castigation of democracies abroad, the assassination of freedom, and such other qualities of the Power State are never subtle."* [160]

Afghanistan was threatened with Communism, as Russia invaded the country in December, 1979. Because the United States opposes

---

158 <u>German Psychological Warfare</u> by Ladislas Farago, 1942, p. 128

159 <u>I Will Bear Witness</u> by Victor Klemperer, 1999, p. 343

160 <u>Men and Power</u> by Henry J. Taylor, 1946, p. 241

the spread of Communism, America began to help Afghanistan in this war. The U.S. and Saudi Arabia each sent as much as $600 million per year to Muslim militant groups in the 1980's, in the form of weaponry, to try to drive the Soviets out of Afghanistan. The Soviets warred in order to set up a Communist government there, which would have been simply another form of Fascist evil. Russia was defeated militarily in Afghanistan by a coalition of forces and went home in 1989.

But in the process of sending aid in the form of weapons, many of the American small arms delivered via neighboring Pakistan by the U.S. Central Intelligence Agency (CIA) were stolen and sold to various drug lords and tribes.[161] Afghan tribal warlords ended up working for radical Muslim terrorist networks. The terrorists ability to conduct jihad was greatly improved by profits from exporting heroin made from Afghan poppies. At the same time, these Muslim terrorists trained jihadists for holy war against the enemies of Islam, first and foremost Israel and America!

Because the Washington administration wanted a friendly state in Afghanistan, which is on the northwest side of Pakistan, America actually supported the rise of the Taliban[162], a Muslim fundamentalist movement in Afghanistan.[163] Russia was driven out of Afghanistan, but support for the Taliban came back to haunt America with the terrorist atttacks of September 11, 2001.

---

161 Jihad: The Trail of Political Islam by Gilles Kepel, 2002, p. 143
162 Ibid., p. 11
163 https://en.wikipedia.org/wiki/Taliban

In 1994, when the Taliban started as a fundamental Islamic political movement, there was the question of constructing a new pipeline for Afghanistan oil. Several American oil companies were involved with the proposal to build it. The Clinton Administration wanted the pipeline run through Pakistan, rather than a shorter route through Iran, because Iran was an enemy of the United States. However, women's rights groups began to threaten withdrawing their support for the 1996 re-election of Bill Clinton if the pipeline was built, because of the extreme human rights violations against women by the Taliban in Afghanistan. The proposed pipeline was never built.[164]

The Taliban, became very wealthy from the heroin drug trade from Afghan poppies, and began waging civil war in Afghanistan in 1995. Other support for the Taliban's struggle came from different Muslim sects. Pakistan (Shia), Saudi Arabia (Sunni), as well as Osama bin Laden's own terrorist group, Al-Qaeda, helped the Taliban by supplying warriors from other Arab nations.

During the Taliban's Afghanistan rule from 1996-2001, scores of Afghan civilians were killed by the Taliban. They also stopped United Nations food shipments intended for 160,000 victims of starvation, and burned crops and thousands of homes. Their aim was, as with other Muslim radicals, supremacy in the Muslim world according to their own doctrines and rules.

American military presence is <u>clearly resented</u> by many Muslim countries and Muslim forces. What Muslims do not grasp is that the United States is intent on tracking down Muslim terrorists and

---

164 <u>Jihad: The Trail of Political Islam</u> by Gilles Kepel, 2002, p. 12

terrorist groups and eliminating them. Therefore, if terrorists were not harbored or trained in a given country, the United States would not invade that country to rectify the problem.

One month after America was attacked by Muslim terrorists in September, 2001, the United States committed combat troops in Afghanistan, to drive the Taliban from power, because of its terrorist connections with the attacks of the New York World Trade Center and the Pentagon in Washington, D. C. This troop commitment in Afghanistan turned out to be America's longest war, lasting 13 years and officially ending on December 28, 2014. The Taliban still exists in remote portions of the country, but they are not in control of the government--for the time being.

True to form, with the alleged withdrawal, America has left thousands of U.S.-led NATO troops behind to train and advise Afghan government forces in this very unstable, Muslim country. The continued involvement of western nation's military forces is a constant provocation of militant Islamic groups. Fascism grows fastest and best in unstable environments such as Afghanistan where crime, violence and drugs are immensely powerful and the government weak.

But, America has yet to learn how fast the players and situations can change with politically motivated Fascist causes, whether they be Communism or Islamic terrorism. The money expended and the American military casualties suffered from over 30 years of involvement in the unstable Muslim country of Afghanistan has to make one wonder whether our efforts have been short sighted if not totally wasted.

In a free society, people work because each has a reasonable expectation that in the future they themselves and their family can gain a better life. The worker does not depend on political affiliations or a labor commissar that must be pleased in order for him to buy or secure a home or a plot of land or whatever it is that he seeks. Freedom and self-interest are parts of this productive equation in life, liberty and the pursuit of individual happiness.

But life under Fascism, which is totalitarian rule, is much different:

"The fascist worship of battle is a suicidal drive, it is a love of death instead of life. In the same idiom, to triumph in battle over the forces which are fighting for death is--again literally--to triumph over death." [165]

Fascism spells war. It leads to war. The following description fits today's insufferable, militant Islam:

" But in the totalitarian state, where bureaucracy, red tape, arbitrariness, politics, party favoritism, and regimentation sooner or later undermine every worker's hopes for the future, and result in squirrel-cage toil, the majority of men and women grow discouraged over the prospect of rewards much beyond the subsistence level. The leaders find that the people work hard and constantly only if taught to fear the future. Production plans in a 'planned economy' do not go well when the leader talks of international tranquility. They go better when the leader tells the people that enemies 'encircle' them,

---

165 <u>The Battle is the Payoff</u> by Ralph Ingersoll, 1943, p. 217

that the nation is surrounded by demons who wish to hurt her, that all sacrifices must be borne, not because the state planners' economic plans are failing but because their lives are at stake as a result of foreign factors beyond the leader's control. The Fascist or Communist states, in the stupidity of their economic concepts, lead directly to the necessity for warmongering." [166]

War, then, is the only way to perpetuate bad political ideologies, such as Fascism. And with Islam, a country simply behaving according to the norms of its own beliefs and customs can be, in the eyes of the Islamist, a crime warranting Islamic jihad against them. This is because in Muslim subjective doctrine, if a society is deemed to be "impious" it is automatically excommunicated from the faith of Islam and considered the enemy of Islam. [167] Under that pretense, there is not a nation on the earth which is not capable of being so accused by one Muslim faction or another.

nry J. Taylor, 1946, p. 244
rail of Islam by Gilles Kepel, 2002, p. 258

CHAPTER 8

Fascism and
mystic powers

———

EVEN BEFORE WORLD WAR ONE, Germans were being influenced by writers, scientists, and politicians, such as historian Albrecht Wirth, who claimed the superiority of German peoples:

"Our hope and faith is that in the future universal domination will belong to Germany" [168]

Fritz Bley, a founder of the Pan-German League, wrote thus of Germany during the reign of Adolf Hitler (though **all** of the following were proven false by the defeat of Hitler's Germany):

"We are the most efficient nation in all spheres of knowledge and the fine arts. We are the best colonists, the best seamen, yes, even the best merchants." [169]

---

168 <u>Is Germany Incurable?</u> by Dr. Richard Brickner, M.D. 1943, p. 168
169 Ibid., p. 169

Kaiser Wilhelm II was the ruler of Germany when it attacked Belgium in 1914, precipitating the First World War. He was a megalomaniac akin to Adolf Hitler and today's Islam. Below is a speech he gave to his armies in 1914. After reading it, read it again substituting the word "**Muslim**" for "**German(s)**" and "**Allah**" for the words "**God**" or "**the Lord**", and the speech sounds precisely like a militant Islamic speech of today:

> *"Remember that you are the chosen people! The spirit of the Lord has descended upon me, because I am Emperor of the Germans! I am the instrument of the Most High. I am His sword, His representative. Woe and death to those who do not believe in my mission! Woe and death to the cowards! May all the enemies of the German people perish! God demands their destruction, God, who through my mouth, commands you to execute His will."* [170]

Germany lost World War One. Unfortunately for the world, Germany in the 1930's, as a nation, followed another megalomaniac in Adolf Hitler. It was a revenge rematch of World War One. As described by one author, the mood in Germany was to make war. This was written before Hitler turned some of his armed forces eastward against Russia:

> *"Here, then, was the German aggressor, back again: a strange and determined reality, challenging all except the new Russian power state. Equally evident, here were Germany's neighbors in western Europe who had handled their own affairs so badly*

---

170 Ibid., p. 181

that they were incompetent to maintain Europe at peace or to supply the men, money and material to stop the Germans at war. That was the meaning of Goering when I saw him, in 1939. "Europe will welcome the Fuehrer," he said. "Europe is Ours." [171]

Heinrich Himmler, Nazi Gestapo Chief, who committed suicide with a hidden cyanide capsule upon his capture by Allied Forces in 1945, published a weekly SS paper during the war, called Das Schwarze Korps. In an effort to create a new religion not unlike their Axis power Japan that was wrapped around the Hitler 'Der Fuhrer' cult. Himmler's SS paper on November 25, 1943, published articles in which the German and the Japanese faiths were discussed and compared at length which stated:

"We have often during this war admired our courageous and heroic ally in the Far East. We have envied him his creed, in which God and his people, according to their mythical origin, are a unity, and according to which every single Japanese knows himself to be eternally reborn after his death and raised to become a Godlike hero"..."As the souls of the dead loved ones do not cease to participate in life here on earth, the souls of the imperial forefathers, too, take part in it." [172]

Free people of this earth value highly the life that they now live. But Fascists teach their sorry subjects that their lives matter little.

By way of example, consider how armies deploy their soldiers in battle. In World War Two, Communist Russia placed little

171 <u>Men and Power</u> by Henry J. Taylor, 1946, p. 24
172 <u>The Nazis Go Underground</u> by Curt Riess, 1944, p. 190

value on the lives of their own soldiers. Russian armies suffered unnecessary loss of life by forced suicidal tactics. The great Russian General Zhukov sent Russian infantry troops marching through buried German mine fields to explode them. Zhukov stated, "If we come to a minefield, we attack exactly as if it were not there."[173]

Conversely, American armies used heavy tanks with mechanical devices to explode mines in their path, in order to preserve the lives of American soldiers in the battle. Eisenhower remarked about this major difference in strategy regarding preserving soldier's lives:

> *"Americans assess the cost of war in terms of human lives, the Russians in the over-all drain on the nation. The Russians clearly understood the value of morale, but for its development and maintenance they apparently depended upon overall success and upon patriotism, possibly fanaticism. As far as I could see, Zhukov had given little concern to methods that we considered vitally important to the maintenance of morale among American troops..."*[174]

It is a well known Koranic promise that Islamic warriors today are promised supposed future rewards after death, for killing and being killed for their god Allah:

> *"Allah has purchased from the believers their lives and properties; for that they will have Paradise. They fight in the cause of Allah, so they kill and are killed."(9:11)*

---

173 <u>Red Army Resurgent</u> by John Shaw, 1979, p. 111
174 <u>Crusade in Europe</u> by Dwight D. Eisenhower, 1948, p. 468

Human life is cheap according to Islamic ideology, as with other Fascist ideologies. The Koran instructs Muslims to die now, get rewarded later. This future payoff means their god Allah purchases men's lives on credit! Where is the proof of the future reward offered? There is none. Non-Muslims love life. Muslims love death by design of their own creed.

It is as empty a sales pitch to right thinking people, as the Nazis pitch for German soldiers to fight and die for the greater glory of the Third Reich!

Special note: The LORD, the Christian God, conversely, testified that He would purchase the souls of His followers with the blood of His own Son Jesus Christ, who came to earth in the form of a man, was tortured and died a violent death. Jesus himself paid the price for sins, that those who believe in Him won't have to pay. What has Allah done for his followers? Answer: nothing!

The stakes are much higher than most people realize in opposing Fascism. This is because the goal of Fascist causes is world wide domination. If mystical, religious flavor can be thrown in to the mix, so much the better for concealing its purposes! Consider Nazi Germany in World War Two:

> *"Even thoughtful Americans had gone to war with only a secondhand or a presumptive case against the Fascist philosophy. Some journalists, a popular President, a few college professors and a politician or two had told them what Fascism meant-- and which way the road led that began with anti-Semitism. But the evidence is that not many Americans really believed*

them. Certainly few really believed what they were told had happened to Germany after only ten years of Fascism--few put any real stock in the fact that the Germans had created a true slave state and were bent on molding the world in its image." [175]

The same author explains in simple terms why America had to go to war against Fascism in 1941:

"Someone should also tell them that there was a reason why they went to France, a reason really good enough to die for. The reason was the Fascist idea, which came so close to prevailing and would have prevailed--but for them. It was there complete in central Europe, and I'm sure also in Japan. If the Fascist states had prevailed--and but for the armed forces of America, they would have--for without us the Chinese, the British and the Russians could not have stopped them--if the Fascists had beaten us, as surely as night follows day their corruption would have spread over the whole world." [176]

Islam seeks control over the world, the same as Germany's Hitler and Japan's Emperor. World control of government is the goal. It matters not whether the ideology is the supposed superiority of a race (German) or a religion (Islam). Fascism is the overriding idea--control of the masses.

Muslims believe that "god" created mankind and let him shift for himself for thousands of years, finally revealing himself to one person, deemed their prophet (Mohammed) in the seventh century A.D.:

---

175 Top Secret by Ralph Ingersoll, 1946, p. 338
176 Top Secret by Ralph Ingersoll, 1946, p. 340-341

" God spoke to one man, and one man only out there in the sand dunes when he dictated "The Reading": al-Qur'an. Since this is the one and only time God spoke to man since the universe began, and since He chose to use the language of the desert dwellers of the day, at that instant that particular desert dialect froze as solid and immutable as the Ka'aba itself in Holy Mecca." [177]

Militant Islamists all over the world have been on a rampage for years, to destroy historic monuments, buildings and other edifices of other cultures and religions. Muslims destroy them because they declare such things to be idols. In February, 2013, the Taliban went to work in Afghanistan:

"This week, officials confirmed that up to 2,000 manuscripts at Mali's Ahmed Baba Institute had been destroyed or looted during a 10-month occupation of Timbuktu by Islamist fighters. Some experts have compared the texts to the Dead Sea Scrolls.

To many in the West, such actions are simply wanton vandalism. However, experts say the thinking behind it is actually part of a wider tradition of rooting out idol-worship and superstition found in Christianity and Judaism as well as Islam." [178]

Herein lies the megalomania and hypocrisy of Islam. While Islam seeks the destruction of so-called idols or relics of other cultures

---

177 http://www.infowars.com/what-does-isis-really-stand-for/

178 http://worldnews.nbcnews.com/_news/2013/02/02/16788304-why-extreme-is-lamists-are-intent-on-destroying-cultural-artifacts?lite

and religions, the Islamic religion is centered on superstition in venerating and worshipping an inanimate object: a rock idol called the Black Stone.

The Black Stone is the cornerstone of a building called the Kaaba. The Kaaba is a small, square black building in the Grand Mosque of Mecca. Mecca is the city in Saudi Arabia where Mohammed, the founder of Islam lived after he conquered the city militarily. This Grand Mosque is considered the most holy site in Islam. All Muslims are commanded to face the city of Mecca when they pray, from anywhere on the planet. (Jews were admonished to pray toward Jerusalem by their king Solomon long before, in about 1005 B.C.)

One might assume this is where their alleged god lives. But remember, any word spoken against the tenets of the Muslim religion or questioning what they believe can never be seriously considered as anything but blasphemy. Fascists have always insisted on everyone seeing things their way and brook no opposition to what they do.

Muslims not only pray facing Mecca, they are urged to visit what they regard as their most holy shrine in the city of Mecca, Saudi Arabia, once in their lifetime. Muslims believe that a pilgrimage to the Grand Mosque in Mecca is tantamount to salvation.

Armed conflict in 1987 in the Grand Mosque of Mecca resulted in the deaths of over 400 people. This came about as Iranian (Shia) Muslims were thought to be trying to take over the Grand Mosque of Mecca, guarded and overseen by Saudis who are Sunni

Muslims. The Iranians were not successful in their attempt to take over the mosque.

As a consequence of the 1987 violence, pilgrimages to Mecca, Saudi Arabia are now granted by Saudi Arabia to other nations strictly by Muslim population. One Muslim pilgrim per thousand Muslim population are allowed to visit the Mecca Grand Mosque each year. Iran has since boycotted Mecca entirely. [179] About two million pilgrims come to Mecca each year, so with 1.6 billion Muslims in the world, most Muslims never reach Mecca.

While visiting the Grand Mosque of Mecca, Muslims are supposed to walk around the Kaaba building seven times in a counterclockwise direction. With each circuit around, Muslims are directed to touch the cornerstone (the Black Stone). If a person is unable to touch or kiss the Black Stone, he or she is to point their right hand at it. (This circumlocution mimics something that happened two thousand years before Mohammed lived. It was what the Jewish nation did in about 1450 B.C., walking around the city of Jericho seven times before the city's walls fell down before them by the power of the LORD their God.)

Islamic tradition holds that the Black Stone fell down from heaven as a guide to the first humans, Adam and Eve, to build an altar. The Christian Bible dates the creation of Adam and Eve at about 4,000 B. C., and makes no mention of any Black Stone or altar constructed by the two first humans. How this

179 <u>Jihad: The Trail of Political Islam</u> by Gilles Kepel, 2002, p. 135

alleged Black Stone from heaven was preserved, discovered and revered by Mohammed over 4,500 years later is left to each person's imagination.

But in the religion of Islam, certain benefits theoretically and magically accrue to those who come to adore and worship this mystic Black Stone. It must be added that the Kaaba building which holds the Black Stone pre-dates Islam. It was alleged to contain 360 idols pertaining to the worship of ancient Mecca gods. It was also associated with earlier fertility rites in Arabia.[180]

So, while Muslims destroy the elements of other religions icons, allegedly to end idol worship, the Islamic religion itself is squarely centered on mysticism and idol worship.

Violent conflicts arise between Muslim sects and terror groups. Iran dominates Shi'ite or Shia Muslims. Saudi Arabia dominates Sunni Muslims. Sunnis and Shi'ites have different doctrines, and each wants their particular brand of Islam to be THE voice of Islam in the world. Each claims to be the only true Islam.

A Sunni Muslim terrorist group calling itself ISIS is today conducting war in the middle east, with the goal of annexing many Islamic countries into one Islamic nation. ISIS in English, means The Islamic State in Iraq and Syria, but in Arabic it means "The Islamic State in Iraq and Ash-Sham", defined as Syria, Cyprus, Turkey, Lebanon, Iraq, Transjordan and Palestine including Israel. Prior to colonization by Britain and France, all these countries were

---

180 https://en.wikipedia.org/wiki/Black_Stone

one under various empires like the Ottomans and Byzantines, as far back as 2,500 years B.C.[181]

ISIS is the terrorist organization which commits mass murders of civilians in its wake, operates female sex slave markets, and is the chief competitor of the Shi'ite Muslim terrorist nation of Iran for top dog in the militant Muslim world. ISIS now controls parts of Iraq and Syria, and has seized oil wells which are providing about $1 million per day to purchase arms and equipment. ISIS versus Iran means Muslims killing Muslims. Other threatened nations are thrown into the fight against ISIS. As of early 2015, a coalition of Jordanian, Saudi, Egyptian, and Iraqi forces have joined Iranian troops in battle against ISIS.[182] Since the 2015 Muslim terrorist attack in Paris, France and Britain have joined the fray.

America is supplying arms to so-called Syrian "rebels" which just happen to be another Muslim terrorist group vying for their continued existence, and reputed to be the Al-Qaeda group. Thus it is that the political situation in the Mideast is both fluid and unstable, exacerbated by politicians in Washington, D.C. who pursue military affiliations with friend and foe alike without regard to long term consequences.

But regardless of which Muslim terrorist group or terrorist State comes out on top, remember that the goal of Islam is Islamic control of the world: religious, legal, political and social! Whether

---

181 http://www.infowars.com/what-does-isis-really-stand-for/

182 http://observer.com/2015/03/saudi-arabia-jordan-and-egypt-unify-to-battle-isis-is-iran-next/

a philosophical or a religious Fascist agenda is used to master nations, totalitarianism is the end product:

> *"National loyalties, they say, should be discarded as 'innovations' and a harsh sharia law should be imposed...Adherents to other religions, 'infidels' will be put in their proper place--that is, into the status of second and third class citizens--or expelled or killed. Ultimately, a pan-Islamic state would unite all Muslims and lead to the restoration of a great Islamic empire--recreating that time when the Prophet and his successors swept through the world."* [183]

---

183 <u>Endgame: The Blueprint for Victory in the War on Terror</u> by Lt. Gen. T. McInerney & Maj. Gen. P. Vallely, 2004, pp. 164-165

CHAPTER 9

Hatred of capitalism and freedom

—

HITLER'S FASCISM, CALLED NATIONAL SOCIALISM (Nazism), dictated the disbanding of all unions in Germany. The regime declared itself the owner of all but a few large companies in Germany. Control of what virtually every enterprise produced under Hitler was announced for the "greater good of the Reich." A war time economy ensued, as Hitler grew Germany's armed strength for waging war. Payment for producing war goods was often in worthless Nazi coupons, rather than German marks.

All worker's occupations and employers were strictly dictated by the Fuehrer and his henchmen. Wages were also set by the government. Deductions from wages were taken for exorbitant taxes to produce yet more war goods. Those deductions included credits earned by workers toward a promised Volkswagen automobile for every family for just $396.00--but not one was ever built![184]

---

[184] <u>The Rise and Fall of the Third Reich</u>, by William L.Shirer, 1960, p.265-267

After Berlin was reduced to rubble by Russian armies in World War Two, survivors certainly saw no automobiles then either. Berliners who survived the onslaught were forced to bring their few possessions with them wherever they roamed, as most Berlin apartments and homes had no doors, no window glass, and at least one wall missing. So, people dragged wooden carts with them through town, which were sarcastically called "Volkswagens."[185]

Diets were strictly controlled, barely above subsistence for civilians. Coupons were issued for the purchase of food, and the penalty for cheating was death. Freedom of speech and freedom of the press were abolished. Western journalists in Germany and German-occupied nations had to submit all news to Nazi propaganda officials before dissemination. They soon learned that truth was of no interest to the Nazi's. Many journalists were incarcerated or expelled from Germany for promulgating truth.

Paris, France endured Nazi Germany occupation for over four years, from June 14, 1940 until August 25, 1945 when American, British and French forces drove the Germans out and continued to drive German armed forces eastward, back to their homeland. German Fascism was, as any Fascism is, a detriment to all affected by its poisonous ways. While France was occupied, much of the food, the industrial output, and French manpower were commandeered by the Nazis and sent to Germany for building weaponry for its armed forces. Hundreds of hotels became Nazi troop rest camps. Capitulation to Fascists brings poverty, disease, fear, want,

---

185 The Candy Bombers by Andrei Cherny, 2008, p. 320

robbery, unhappiness, broken families, rape, enslavement, torture, executions, and many other crimes of war because Fascism **is** war:

> *"All Europe is a single interminable bread line. Women stand in line for hours. They wait in the broiling heat, they wait in the freezing cold, they stay in line, knowing that they will get little today, that they will get less tomorrow, they will get less and less as time goes on. The women of Paris wait in a long queue. They need milk for their children. Their children are pale, almost transparent; at night they cannot sleep for hunger. The women of Paris are clamoring for milk.*
>
> *The women of Oslo are waiting in front of Jensen & Co.'s store. Jensen & Co. have installed a new counter laden with plenty of butter, eggs, and cheese. The counter is for Germans only. The Norwegian women have to wait at their particular counter. They wait a long time, and when finally their turn comes, nothing is left. The clerk says, 'come early tomorrow, there may be something then.' The Norwegian women go home. Tears do not come easily to the women of Norway."* [186]

Fascism brings financial ruin. The financial plunder of western Europe by Hitler's Germany was incalculable:

> *"A great deal was taken out, not only in goods and services but in banknotes and gold. Whenever Hitler occupied a country, his financial agents seized the gold and foreign holdings of its national bank. That was a mere beginning. Staggering "occupation costs" were immediately assessed. By the end of February, 1944, Count Schwerin von Krosigk, the Nazi*

---

186 <u>Underground Europe</u> by Curt Riess, 1942, p. 232

Minister of Finance, put the total take from such payments at some 48 billion marks (roughly $12 billion), of which France, which was milked heavier than any other conquered country, furnished more than half." [187]

Another example of control that Fascism exercises in a society, was written by a French woman who managed to survive a Nazi labor camp. The camp was inhabited by 22,000 women of various nationalities who were ordered at gunpoint onto German trains from the countries Nazi Germany overran:

"We were marshalled into an immense hall, where we remained standing, panting, amidst our bags and our bundles. There were two doors in the wall facing us. One at a time, each of us was pushed through the door on the right. The woman who passed through that door was just an ordinary person, carrying her bags and her coat and wearing her everyday clothes. We heard screams and abuses in German. Presently, through the other door, a naked woman appeared, empty-handed, her head shaved. Things happened fast behind those doors: a moment to set the bags down, to undress quickly, hastened on by hands that reached out to tear the clothing off...'Schnell, schnell.' Slaps were landing right and left and abusive language exploding all around us." [188]

Wealthy and famous people are sometimes duped by Fascism. The wealthy and the famous do not lend credibility to the ideology of Fascism! For example, the richest and most powerful

---

187 <u>The Rise and Fall of the Third Reich</u>, by William L.Shirer, 1960, p. 943
188 <u>An Ordinary Camp</u> by Micheline Maurel, 1958, p. 2

industrialist in Germany who actually supported Adolf's Hitler in his plans to come to rule the country with National Socialism, got a rude awakening. His name was Fritz Thyssen, owner of coal mines and the largest steel maker in Germany. Mr. Thyssen protested the treatment of the Catholic church because he himself was Catholic. He also expressed opposition to making war against Poland.

As a result, Thyssen became an enemy of the state. He fled from Germany for his life, with his wife and children. His steel works, his home, his bank accounts and his citizenship were all taken away as the Nazi Fascists declared Thyssen to be a traitor to the Third Reich.[189] Thyssen's Austrian nephew was not so fortunate, and was arrested and thrown into the Nazi concentration camp at Dachau, where he died.

Likewise, during the era of World War Two, Nazi spies and fifth column agents conducted a war of propaganda in America, criticizing aid to Britain, protesting the build-up of our armed forces as the world war erupted. These efforts to subvert America into support for Nazi Germany were always hidden behind patriotic sounding organizational names, such as the "America First" campaign which heralded the famous transatlantic flight hero Charles Lindbergh as a proponent of staying out of the war.

Through patriotic sounding messages, money was raised from major corporations such as Republic Steel, Hormel, Allis-Chalmers, the Chicago Tribune, the New York Daily News, Quaker Oats and

---

189 I Paid Hitler by Fritz Thyssen, 1941, pp. 44-57

others. Henry Ford himself contributed $300,000. to the America First Committee.[190]

Henry Ford also owned the hometown newspaper in Dearborn, Michigan called <u>The Dearborn Independent</u>. Henry Ford was ardently against labor unions, and had many conflicts with his own workers, that even resulted in the beatings and killings of his workers by company security forces. Since National Socialism stood for outlawing labor unions, it is no surprise that Henry Ford was duped about National Socialism in total.

Henry Ford's Dearborn newspaper had published numerous anti-Semitic articles for seven years in the 1920's. Though he apologized in 1927 for these articles and suspended the newspaper, the damage was done. The newspaper articles against Jews were reprinted endlessly throughout the Great Depression and on through the Second World War. [191]

Due to the seditious literature and speeches of the America First Committee, the organization was outlawed and disbanded by the Attorney General of the United States. Many of its principal leaders (some were German or Russian) were convicted of sedition against the United States and either deported, imprisoned and/or citizenship revoked.

National Socialism (Nazism), spawned in Germany under Hitler, was Fascist. Some people are not aware that Henry Ford was a Socialist, which helps explain his aversion to labor unions

---

190 <u>Under Cover</u> by John Roy Carlson, 1943, p. 244
191 <u>Under Cover</u> by John Roy Carlson, 1943, p. 208

which he fought against unsuccessfully at Ford Motor Company. His socialistic beliefs are alive and well today embodied in the Ford Foundation. This huge nonprofit corporation, established by Henry Ford, and perpetuated in part by Ford Motor Company's contributions, donates money under the guise of supporting human rights around the globe. But in reality, the contributions go to the most radical, undemocratic social causes in existence today.

The Ford Foundation has funded meetings in various parts of the world, for the "World Social Forum," a socialist organization founded in 2001 to advocate such things as America paying reparations for negro slavery, taxation of all investment transactions worldwide, and reinventing democracy through the imposition of political power for every level of society in accordance with Communist principles. The Ford Foundation contributed $500,000. for the 2003 meeting, which assisted 500 American non-governmental delegates to attend from such interests as Ralph Nader's Public Citizen organization. World Social Forum speakers have included the pro-Castro presidents of Venezuela and Brazil.[192]

Is it any wonder, then, that Dearborn, Michigan, a city of 100,000 people now has the largest Muslim population of any city in America, some 40,000 Muslims. The city has no fewer than five sizeable Muslim mosques. And trouble is brewing in Dearborn between Muslims and non-Muslims. Incidences of violence are growing. The 6th Circuit U.S. Court of Appeals is reviewing a First Amendment complaint brought by Christians who were attacked by a rock-throwing Muslim mob at an Arab festival in Dearborn,

---

192 <u>Unholy Alliance</u> by David Horowitz, 2004, p. 158-161

Michigan, in 2012, and then ordered to leave the festival by Wayne County Sheriff's deputies.[193] An earlier attack on Christians by Muslims at the annual Arab festival there resulted in an award of $100,000. to the injured people.

The Religious Freedom Coalition reports that hate crimes are on the rise in Dearborn, Michigan, such as the physical assault of a high school football player by four Muslim teenagers whose Muslim high school was soundly defeated in a football game with a Christian high school. They reported:

> *"Dearborn is now majority Muslim and the Muslim children are taught they are superior to infidels in all things and that violence against infidels is always justified by the Qur'an."* [194]

Nazi Germany largely used racial hatred and intolerance to build its Fascist empire. The Muslim world likewise uses racial hatred and intolerance under the banner of their religion, to foster their goal of world domination. Islam does not tolerate freedom of religion or speech, nor expression of opinion. The freedoms extended to Muslims in the United States today, would in no way continue to be offered the whole citizenry when and if Muslims came to political governance of our nation.

It is the nature of fascists to demand for themselves the liberties they desire, while at the same time their intent is to deny

---

193 http://www.wnd.com/2014/10/christians-bloodied-by-stone-throwing-muslims-in-michigan/

194 http://www.religiousfreedomcoalition.org/2012/01/27/hate-crime-violence-by-muslims-on-upswing-in-michigan/

those same liberties were they to be elevated to be in charge and bear rule! For instance, Hitler's Minister of Propaganda, Dr. Joseph Goebbels, explained just how Nazi Fascism operated:

> *"We National Socialists have never maintained that we were representatives of a democratic viewpoint, but we have openly declared that we only made use of democratic means in order to gain power, and that after the seizure of power we would ruthlessly deny to our opponents all those means which they had granted to us during the time of our opposition."* [195]

Such is the case with Sharia law, which Muslims would impose today worldwide if they were able to do so. The free world must not feign blindness to the aims of Islamic Fascism. Personal freedoms of speech and religion are nonexistent in Islamic-ruled nations. Possessing a Christian Bible in a Muslim-ruled nation is tantamount to death as an enemy of Allah (the god of Mohammedism, the religion now called Islam or Muslim). Daniel Berg, a Jewish reporter for the Wall Street Journal newspaper, was kidnapped and beheaded by Muslims and a film taken of his murder, made available on the world wide web for all to see what Islam will do to all enemies of their savage, Satanic so-called "religion" if they could get away with it. Public beheadings by Muslim terrorists are increasingly commonplace.

Does this seem savage to the average human being today, to behead a person who has committed no crime, and to film the bloody

---

195 <u>Under Cover</u> by John Roy Carlson, 1943, p. 499

deed? This ghastly violence is precisely why Islam mirrors Nazi Fascism. Germany also committed unspeakable acts of savagery:

> *"Not only skeletons but human skins were collected by the masters of the New Order though in the latter case the pretense could not be made that the cause of scientific research was being served. The skins of concentration camp prisoners, especially executed for this ghoulish purpose, had merely decorative value. They made, it was found, excellent lamp shades, several of which were expressly fitted up for Frau Ilse Koch, the wife of the commandant of Buchenwald and nicknamed by the inmates the 'Bitch of Buchenwald.' Tattooed skins appear to have been the most sought after."* [196]

---

196 <u>The Rise and Fall of the Third Reich</u>, by William L.Shirer, 1960, p. 983-984

CHAPTER 10

Fascists diminishing
of women

———

SOUND MORALS AND MORALITY PRODUCE a healthy society. Marriage is the basic building block of a civil nation. The dignity of one man married to one woman for life involves many positive attributes that enhance the righteousness and character of a nation and its people. Relationships are more permanent, personal conduct more honorable and accountable, and neighborhoods, towns and nations are more stable, healthy and productive.

The opposite is true when the morals of a nation are vile. The United States Supreme Court has adjudged its verdict changing the definition of the word marriage, which has always had but one meaning--in favor of sexual perversity. And by opening the door legally as to who a person can marry, the Court has opened the floodgates to the eventual accession to the issue of how many persons one can marry. This plays directly into the hands of perverse ideologies developing and spreading, such as polygamous Islam.

Expect trouble when age-old, tried and true moral codes are broken or set aside.

Marriage is an irreplaceable bond between a man and a woman. How disrespectful of decency and honor toward women is the case of a man who would cohabitate with a woman without marriage, and beget children with a woman who has not been given the honor and protection of the bond of matrimony? How much respect could a child have toward his parents if the father has several wives? Polygamy also dishonors women. The uprightness of entire nations can be judged by the morals or lack thereof in its family structures.

Polygamous Muslims will point out how some of the patriarchs in the Old Testament of the Holy Bible had multiple wives, in justifying the common practice among themselves. But the Bible makes it quite clear that the LORD, God and Creator of heaven and earth, gave clear instruction to mankind against polygamy.

As Jesus Christ, the virgin born Son of God told the Jewish officials who asked him about marriage, He told them "..Have ye not read, that he which made them at the beginning made them male and female, And said, For this cause shall a man leave father and mother, and shall cleave to his wife: and they twain shall be one flesh? Wherefore they are no more twain, but one flesh. What therefore God hath joined together, let not man put asunder." (Matthew 19: 4-6, King James Bible) Notice the instruction is NOT to cleave to wives, but to one wife.

Nazi Germany Fascist immorality
toward women

Nazi Germany promulgated widely a national program which urged unmarried women to have sexual intercourse without marriage in order to produce more babies for what was claimed to be the superior race of people on the earth. The goal was to allow Germany to reign over all the countries of the world, and for that more good Nazis were going to be needed.

It was the stated goal of Adolf Hitler to bring the population of the German Reich from 80 million Aryans to 120 million by the year 1980.[197] Thus, Nazi Heinrich Himmler brought forth the Lebensborn, or "Fountain of Life" program. State ministries and Nazi party leaders persuaded young German women that they were "racially valuable" and that they should have offspring out of wedlock.

Birthing centers were established, and infant child care as well as foster parents provided for thousands of such children fathered mostly by German Army officers, especially the brutal SS officers. Generous off-duty leaves were given to officers to perform their patriotic procreative duty. New mothers were allowed to be called "Mrs." even if they were unmarried, further mocking marriage. Birth certificates were furnished by the State, and propaganda messages broadcast by radio to all Germany that made it a crime to speak ill of any young woman for having children outside of the bonds of marriage.[198] The unfortunate offspring in this case is another dark side of Fascist's lust for power.

---

197 <u>The Nazis</u> by Robert E. Herzstein, 1980, p. 91
198 Ibid., p. 98

A soft spoken tailor from Potsdam, Germany, was sent to a concentration camp in Esterwege, Germany, and subsequently shot dead as an enemy to the "Fountain of Life" program, because he opposed Hitler's forced pregnancy and childbirth program for unmarried females which operated through so-called "Nazi Girls' Camps":

> *"..his only crime was an understandable reluctance to send his daughter to a Nazi Girls' Camp. When he was questioned by the authorities, he finally blurted out the truth: 'Erna is only 14 years old and I can't bear the idea of her becoming a mother.'"* [199]

NAZI FORCED MARRIAGES AND SEXUAL SLAVERY

During the forced military and civil government occupation of Norway by Hitler's forces, young Norwegian women were forced to marry German soldiers against their will:

> *"The Germans knew no bounds in their efforts to compel love from the Norwegians. Toward the end of 1940 the Cathedral at Trondheim was the scene of an unprecedented spectacle. More than a hundred young women were married to German soldiers with great pomp and circumstance. These young women had not been consulted as to their wishes in the matter. It was a multiple shotgun wedding, except that this time the women were coerced into the ceremony. Nor were the brides consulted afterwards as to where they desired to live. They were cooly informed that they were now German citizens, that they*

---

199 <u>Four Years of Nazi Torture</u> by Ernst Winkler, 1942, p. 113-114

had to keep their mouths shut, and go to Germany. They were given only a few hours to say good-bye to their families." [200]

The corrupt morals of Nazis were not limited to forced marriages. In Poland, outwardly beautiful girls were shipped to Berlin by the Nazis, and then sent to the western front for forced prostitution in a brothel for German army soldiers.[201]

ISLAMIC FASCIST ABUSE OF WOMEN (TO HELP THE CAUSE)

Islamic ideology dictates that men routinely have multiple wives or concubines, just as the Mormon cult practices. So, while the Muslims claim a more moral doctrine with pre-marital sex absolutely forbidden (as with the Christian faith), the polygamy of Islam demonstrates the true immorality of the Islamic cult. For the Muslim, the express intent is both gratifying the desires of men, and greatly increasing the Islamic population worldwide:

" According to Sharia law, Muslims are allowed to practice polygamy. According to the Qur'an, a man may have up to four legal wives at any one time the restriction on the number was not customary before the advent of Islam in Arabia. The husband is required to treat all wives equally. If a man fears that he will not be able to meet these conditions then he is not allowed more than one wife. 'If ye fear that ye shall not be able to deal justly with the orphans, marry women of your choice, two, or three, or four; but if ye fear that ye shall not be able to

---

200 <u>Underground Europe</u> by Curt Riess, 1942, pp. 121-122
201 <u>Underground Europe</u> by Curt Riess, 1942, p. 201

deal justly (with them), then only one, or that which your right hands possess. That will be more suitable, to prevent you from doing injustice.' (Qur'an 4:3) Yusuf Ali translation." [202]

The quote above mentions "that which your right hands possess." The literal meaning of that phrase is, that it is perfectly acceptable to keep sexual slaves. The terror group ISIS sells females in their own sex slave market acquired from women and girls kidnapped by ISIS.[203]

A consequence of polygamy quite naturally is population explosion. Abnormal child development problems develop when children are not raised in a "one man, one woman" bond of marriage. The population explosion of Muslim nations is also fanning the fires of Islamic terrorism!

Terrorist organizer and financier Osama bin Laden, remember, was one of fifty-four children of his wealthy father. This of course means his father had many wives and concubines. Another example of evil in polygamy was Emperor Hirohito, Japan's Fascist ruler in World War Two, who was the offspring of one of his father, Emperor Yoshihito's, many concubines.

The polygamy of Islamists shows some distressing statistics:

1. The world's Muslim population increased by 50% in the fifteen years between 1955 and 1970.[204]

---

202 "Sharia Law: Polygamy" by Wikipedia, the Online Encyclopedia, 2014
203 The Complete Infidel's Guide to ISIS by Robert Spencer, 2015, pp. 156-158
204 Jihad: The Trail of Political Islam by Gilles Kepel, 2002, p. 66

2. In 1991, in the Arab occupied territory of Palestine, hotbed of Muslim-Jewish friction, 70% of the Muslim population was under the age of 30 years.[205]

3. The reproduction rate in the Muslim occupied West Bank and Gaza in 1991 was 8.1 children and 9.8 children respectively for each Muslim woman.[206] (Gaza showed 32 births/1,000 people which is nearly three times the birth rate in western non-Muslim countries. See #5 below.)

4. The population of Pakistan doubled between 1970 and 1990, to 121 million people. By 2010, it grew to 178 million, an increase of almost 50%.[207] The country is 96% Muslim.

5. The average birth rate among the 464 million Shia (Shi'ite) Muslims that constitute the countries of Iran, Iraq, Pakistan and India is 22 births/thousand population. In four large non-Muslim countries of the U.S., France, Britain and Germany the average birth rate is 11 births per thousand people.[208] This information is gathered by the U.S. Central Intelligence Agency.

The Muslim population explosion from polygamy (multiple wives) has fostered economic problems and unrest that dovetail nicely with the Muslim religion which has no problem in using violence to secure what they desire. There is not an economy on earth which can develop as quickly as needed to support full-time

---

205 Ibid., p. 152

206 Ibid., p. 397

207 https://en.wikipedia.org/wiki/Islam_by_country

208 https://www.cia.gov/library/publications/the-world-factbook/rankorder/2054rank.html

employment for such rapid growth of population as Islam has brought due to polygamy and a very high birth rate.

Unemployment is a principal cause of civil unrest and crime among poor, young adult Muslim men. In Muslim countries with majority Muslim populations, unemployment problems are worse, unless the country is a significant oil producer. The economically disadvantaged youths of Muslim countries have been and are recruited for various Muslim extremist groups or factions to war against their own government, or against the latest chosen and demonized enemy. The mobility of Islamic terrorists from one Muslim nation to another has exacerbated the recruitment to wage jihad, so-called holy war.

Algeria, for example, had an unemployment rate of 28% in 1995.[209] Algeria not surprisingly had rioting which began in October, 1988, and turned into a full blown civil war in 1991, which lasted for 12 years. Muslim factions fought for control of Algeria, and it is estimated that somewhere between 40,000-200,000 people died in this civil war.[210] In the fighting, entire villages were massacred. This is Muslim versus Muslim violence. Shia and Sunni Muslim sects have no problem killing one another singly or en-masse, each claiming the exclusive "franchise" to genuine Islam.

Impoverished, urban young adult Muslim men in Algeria joined the brutal fighting because of problems of unemployment and insufficient housing, which problems they were taught to

---

209 Jihad: The Trail of Political Islam by Gilles Kepel, 2002, pp. 152-158
210 https://en.wikipedia.org/wiki/Algerian_Civil_War

expect the government in power should have solved. (Question: Where can a Muslim man with four wives and 32 children live?)

More recently, 2008, the Islamic Republic of Afghanistan, a country of about 29 million people, had an unemployment rate of 35%.[211] The country is 99% Muslim.

ISLAMIC FORCED MARRIAGES AND SEXUAL SLAVERY

Over 220 teenage girls were kidnapped in Lagos, Nigeria in April, 2014, by the Islamic terrorist group known as Boko Haram. The girls were sold into marriage to warriors in the Boko group for about $12.00 each. The Nigerian government admitted it did not possess the military strength to rescue the girls. The mass kidnapping followed a bombing in the capital city which killed more than 70 people and injured scores.[212]

On August 6, 2015 the United Kingdom's Daily Mail newspaper reported the details of the sale of kidnapped Muslim and Christian women for forced marriages in Iraq by the ISIS terrorist group. The ISIS group maintains a "Women and Cattle Market" where women are sold as sexual slaves or wives. The price paid depends on the age of the female. As of October 16, 2014, the price list is as follows:[213]

$43 (£27) for women between the age of 40-50
$75 (48) for women 30 to 40-year-olds

---

211 https://en.wikipedia.org/wiki/List_of_countries_by_unemployment_rate
212 CBS News, April 30, 2014
213 http://www.dailymail.co.uk/news/article-3186229/ISIS-executes-19-girls-refusing-sex-fighters-envoy-reveals-sex-slaves-peddled-like-barrels-petrol.html

$86 (£55) for women 20 to 30-year-olds
$130 (£83) for females ten to 20-year-olds
$172 (£110) for females one to nine-year-olds

ISIS fighters get to choose their purchases first and then wealthy Middle-Easterners are allowed to buy. Females are referred to as items in the ISIS pamphlet which states that customers are allowed to buy only three items except customers from Turkey, Syria and Gulf countries.

A United Nations envoy previously said the best looking Yazidi (Iraqi Muslim) virgins are sent to depraved slave auctions in Islamic State's adopted capital of Raqqa (city of 300,000 people) in Syria, where they are stripped naked and sold to the highest bidder.

The story was verified by humanitarian and peace prize winner Dr Widad Akrawi, and by United Nations special envoy for sexual violence in conflict which reported that females are bought and sold like barrels of oil. Also reported in the story was the execution of 19 women who refused to have sex with their captors.[214]

In France today, the average immigrant Muslim woman births eight children while the ethnic French have two or less. It is no wonder why Paris, France today is reeling from Islamic violence even as a burgeoning Muslim population is further strengthened by mid-east Arabic Muslims continuing to emigrate to France and changing the ethnic landscape by design.

---

214 http://www.dailymail.co.uk/news/article-3186229/ISIS-executes-19-girls-refusing-sex-fighters-envoy-reveals-sex-slaves-peddled-like-barrels-petrol.html

As with any Fascist totalitarian system, Islamic Fascism extends all the way down to the home. Men rule over their wives as though they were slaves. The Quran (Koran) advises men that if they are certain of a rebellious attitude by the woman, they should first admonish her, then refuse to share beds, and finally beat ("darab") her, according to Qur'an 4:34.

Women are literally kept under wraps in the "religion of Islam," covered from head to foot in what essentially looks like a large blanket or bedspread. "The burkha is an enveloping outer garment worn by women in Islamic tradition, to cover their bodies when in public. The face-veiling portion is usually a rectangular piece of semi-transparent cloth with its top edge attached to a portion of the head-scarf so that the veil hangs down covering the face and can be turned up if the woman wishes to reveal her face. In other styles, the niqāb of the veil is attached by one side, and covers the face only below the eyes, allowing the eyes to be seen."[215]

Muslim women in Islamic-ruled countries are governed by Sharia Law. Women are required to be attired in the burkha clothing that covers their entire body including the head, with only slits for the woman to see out. In Iran, the full Islamic dress and veil was made mandatory by law since April, 1983, with strict rules as to the length, shape and colors allowed. Posters in public places boldly lay down this law for all females.[216]

---

215 https://en.wikipedia.org/wiki/burqa
216 Jihad: The Trail of Political Islam by Gilles Kepel, 2002, p. 117

In Pakistan, the practice of "purdah" is observed by many Muslims, which carries the obscurity of females one step further. There, a married Muslim woman is forbidden to ever be seen by a male outside of the immediate family.[217] The role of women in Islam borders on human slavery.

In Afghanistan, in 2001, the Sunni Muslim terrorists were in control of the country. A Muslim woman was seen walking with a man who was not a relative. She was arrested for adultery, and received 100 lashes at a public stadium. The Taliban also ordered all females out of schools.[218]

Malaysia is a country of 30 million people, about two-thirds of them Muslim. The constitution declares Islam as the State religion but allows freedom of religion for non-Muslims. The jurisdiction of Sharia courts was established to govern Muslims by Sharia Law in matters such as marriage, inheritance, divorce, apostasy, religious conversion, and custody among others.[219] As a result, Islamic police in Malaysia can check the marital status of a male and female who happen to be in company, by the electronic identity cards which all citizens aged 12 and older must carry. If a male and female Muslim are found together who are not married, they are subject to arrest and prosecution for the Muslim crime called "khalwa" or consorting illegally.[220] This is carrying the reach of government too far, but emblematic of what to expect if you live in a Muslim-ruled country.

---

217 <u>American Jihad: The Terrorists Living Among Us</u> by Steven Emerson, 2002, p. 65
218 https://en.wikipedia.org/wiki/Taliban
219 https://en.wikipedia.org/wiki/Malaysia
220 <u>Jihad: The Trail of Political Islam</u> by Gilles Kepel, 2002, p. 96

Islamic practices affect laws in non-Muslim countries as well. Because of the constant threat of Islamic suicide bombers in our world today, France enacted a law in 2010 which bans the wearing of the burkha in public, including the public schools. Support came from various quarters which also descried the subjugation of women. The bill was introduced with this description:

> *"Given the damage it produces on those rules which allow the life in community, ensure the dignity of the person and equality between sexes, this practice, even if it is voluntary, cannot be tolerated in any public place"* [221]

The ban is officially called "The bill to forbid concealing one's face in public".[222] This title was chosen expressly to avoid accusations of religious discrimination. In 2014, the law was upheld when challenged, in the European Court of Human Rights. Other western nations will undoubtedly be forced to face this issue due to burkha-disguised suicide bombing attacks, as well as the safety of banking institutions.

What other kinds of restrictions and problems exist for women in Islam? There are many. In Afghanistan, in 2010, U.S. Army soldiers were ordered never to look at or to take a photograph of an Afghanistan female. The reason was that for an Afghan Muslim woman, simply having your picture taken with a non-family male was grounds for the woman to be put on trial for adultery under the Islamic traditions of that country.

---

221 https://en.wikipedia.org/wiki/burqa
222 https://en.wikipedia.org/wiki/burqa

In Syria and Iraq, ISIS controls everyone. Women cannot leave home unless accompanied by a male relative. Sharia patrols lurk in the declared capital city of Raqqa 24 hours a day. One Sharia patrol is for men, and another is on the streets policing for women, to insure that all are in conformance with Islamic law. This means not only clothing, but conduct and even grooming. Beards are required for men. Shops must close and people be in prayer at prescribed times or face arrest and punishment.[223] Does this sound like the kind of place you would like to live?

---

223 The Complete Infidel's Guide to ISIS by Robert Spencer, 2015, pp. 134-135

CHAPTER 11

Punishment for speaking against Fascism

——

NAZI FASCISM TACTICS

THE GERMAN GESTAPO (GERMAN STATE Secret Police) had its operatives in every factory, apartment house, and beer garden both in Germany and amongst the 300 million people under forced Nazi occupation during World War Two. Rewards were paid for turning in people who murmured or complained about any facet of life under the Nazi thumb. If arrested, suspicion of collaboration against Germany brought torture, confiscation of property, and/or internment in a forced labor or concentration (death) camp.

During Hitler's reign, Nazi radio broadcasts throughout Germany regularly warned German citizens that if they were found to be complacent, lazy or unproductive in the job they were given by the State, for turning out German war goods at a feverish pace, they would find themselves in a forced labor camp, which came to be known as death camps or concentration camps.

Just to get the point across, factory foremen or plant managers were instructed to single out a worker from time to time, perhaps one who had complained about working conditions or damaged a product or machine. That worker was sent to a forced labor camp in Germany where the living conditions were so severe that if the worker managed to live the three to six months they were incarcerated there, his return to his former factory in nearly skeletal condition served as the motivator for other German workers in the plant to work very productively lest they suffer the same fate.[224] These formerly incarcerated workers told others what they had seen in the forced labor camps. It was no secret.

Speaking out against the Nazi party was also not tolerated at all. In 1943, Germany had been under Hitler's terrorist regime for ten years. There was an undercurrent of disillusionment with Hitler's rule after the sound defeat and capture of the Sixth German Army at Stalingrad. Consequently, a group of university students at the University of Munich began anti-Nazi student demonstrations openly in the streets of Munich. They also distributed literature denouncing National Socialism.

But this movement was put to an end quickly, as the leaders of the group which called itself the White Rose movement, were arrested, tortured, and brought to trial in the so-called People's Court. They were executed by guillotine for the crime of treason against the Nazi Party which of course was the State.[225]

ISLAMIC FASCIST TACTICS

It is not reality to think that Islam is anything other than violent Fascism. In 1989, the head of the Islamic Republic of Iran,

---

224 <u>The Rise and Fall of the Third Reich</u>, by William L.Shirer, 1960, p. 263-265
225 <u>The Rise and Fall of the Third Reich</u> by William Shirer, 1960, pp. 1022-1023

Ayatollah Khomeini, gave his famous Islamic fatwa or legal opinion condemning to death, an author who had written a book considered insulting to Islam. The author's name is Salman Rushdie, and this fictional book was entitled "Satanic Verses." Khomeini's announcement was tantamount to his claiming global power to pronounce a death sentence against a person. Mr. Rushdie, the author, is a British citizen, not an Iranian. [226] Mr. Rushdie of course had to disappear from ordinary life and now lives in hiding and in fear for the rest of his life.

This presumptuous precedent of Khomeini has become common practice in the Muslim world, to pronounce a death sentence against anyone who speaks or writes against Islam or Mohammed. Keep in mind, an open threat of violence or death against a person in a free society are considered a crime.

Monetary rewards are offered by Muslim authorities or leaders for such killings. Steven Emerson, who wrote the book "American Jihad" in 2002, saw his picture on the front page of an Arabic language newspaper, with the image of a target bulls-eye on his face.[227] He lives a secret and fearful life as well.

In recent years, Dutch cartoonists have poked fun at Mohammed, the alleged prophet of Islam. Those cartoonists were declared to be the enemies of Islam and as such went into hiding for their lives from Islamic terrorists due to death threats. At least one of the cartoonists, Theo Van Gogh, was murdered. Mr. Van

---

226 Jihad: The Trail of Political Islam by Gilles Kepel, 2002, p. 9
227 American Jihad: The Terrorists Living Among Us by Steven Emerson, 2002, p. 14

Gogh was the author of a book critical of Islam and a short film critical of the mistreatment of Muslim women.

Mr. Van Gogh was attacked while riding his bicycle to work in broad daylight in Amsterdam, Netherlands. He was shot eight times and partially beheaded by a Moroccan man named Mohammed _____, (last name purposely omitted) now serving a life sentence in prison for murder. The killer left a written death threat on the body of the victim, naming yet another author, as well as general threats against the West and against Jews.[228]

Hooded Muslim terrorists shot and killed a dozen unarmed people in a small newspaper in Paris, France, in January, 2015 because the newspaper which employed them, poked fun at Islam and their prophet Mohammed. Freedom of speech and thought are foreign to Islam. Muslim leaders are radical extremists for their declared cause. "Death to the enemies of Islam" is consistently the mantra.

FACTIONALISM AMONGST VIOLENT MUSLIM FASCISTS

It is no secret that there is violent hatred between Muslim sects as well as hatred for non-Muslims. Not only do Sunni Muslims and Shia or Shi'ite Muslims conduct jihad against non-Muslims, but each of these two largest sects of the religion also support jihad against each other. Sunni Muslims represent about 80% of all Muslims in the world.[229] Most of the rest of Muslims are Shia

---

228 https://en.wikipedia.org/wiki/Theo_van_Gogh_(film_director)
229 Jihad: The Trail of Political Islam by Gilles Kepel, 2002, p. 120

or Shi'ite Muslims. Each of the two claim to have more of or the entire authentic legacy and genuine beliefs of Mohammed, the founder of Islam.

Saudi Arabia, sometimes called petro-Islam, heads up the Sunni Muslim community primarily by two plain facts. One is the power of its unbelievable oil wealth. Secondly, both Mecca and Medina, "holy sites" of Islam, are located within Saudi Arabia's borders which means they strictly control those sites.

Because Saudis claim their Sunni Islamic faith is the true line and offspring of Islam, and the purest and most conservative, their forces have gone about smashing the tombs of Shia imams (deceased Islamic clerics).[230] There are many other hostilities and conflicts, even open warfare have come about between the Sunni and Shia sects.

An eight year war raged from 1980 until 1988, between the Sunni Muslims of Saddam Hussein's Iraqi armies and the Shia Muslims of neighboring Iran. Iraq had invaded Iran, but the battle was pushed back westward onto Iraqi territory for some time before Iranian forces were finally pushed back eastward out of Iraq and into their own country. A ceasefire was then declared. About 160,000 Iranians died in this long war.[231] Iraq's war dead numbered somewhere between 250,000-500,000.[232]

---

230 Ibid., p. 75
231 https://en.wikipedia.org/wiki/Iran#Religion
232 http://www.theguardian.com/world/2010/sep/23/iran-iraq-war-anniversarypass from memory into history.

Since the State and Islam are one in countries such as Iran and Iraq, young Muslim men gladly give their lives for defeating the enemy. Unfortunately, the huge number of men that died in the Iran-Iraq war helped create the symbolism of martyrdom that now runs through Islam:

> *"The killing of so many young men brought about the symbolic death of their class as a collective political protagonist in Iran... The appalling butchery of the eight year war against Iraq gave the younger generation of poor Iranians an incentive to return to the former tradition of martyrdom, pushing the ritual of self-flagellation to the point of self-immolation--the ultimate sacrifice."* [233]

The Islamic Republic of Iran has the largest Shia population in the world, over 75 million people. Iran's biggest success story in terror has been the creation of the terrorist group Hezbollah, which works to export revolution throughout the poor and disinherited Muslim people of the world such as in Lebanon. [234]

Must the free world give way to the Fascist ideas present with Islamic militants, such as the idea that no one can hold or express an opinion, a thought, or a criticism against Islam? The answer is no. To succumb to the threats of Islam whether open or veiled (no pun intended), simply paves the way for Islam to silence all free speech and thought.

We now know that Muslims are willing to commit suicide as they blow up themselves and others with bombs. But, we must face

---

233 Jihad: The Trail of Political Islam by Gilles Kepel, 2002, p. 116
234 Ibid., p. 130

the threat of Islamic terrorism regardless. Free societies function with the exercise of free speech and thought. These must be continually exercised or succumb to tyrannical powers.

CHAPTER 12

The indoctrination of children

———

NAZI GERMANY'S EXAMPLE

IN HITLER'S GERMANY, STORM TROOPERS had a famous ballad that included the words "We spit on freedom." Children were indoctrinated in schools and camps as part of the Hitler Youth Movement, to unquestionably follow their German leaders pursuing the enemies of National Socialism (Nazism). Boys were taught to prepare for war by being taught the mechanics of many different firearms and weapons of war at an early age.

Alfred Rosenberg, a Nazi ideologist, wrote directives for the mass killing of Jews. His subordinates ruled occupied nations of western Europe with an iron fist and contributed to the literal starvation of millions of people. He was executed by hanging for his part in German crimes against humanity, at the Nuremberg War Trials following World War Two.

Rosenberg also wrote about the indoctrination of German youth:

> " *'Give me ten years and no boy or girl in the Reich will as much as remember what the Sunday school was, let alone attend it.' His plan eliminates the convent and cloister as evil influences; it places the Fatherland and Fuehrer before the altar and God, leaving the latter as a sort of tolerated commodity to be called on for effect whenever the occasion warrants it."* [235]

Alfred Rosenberg contrived the thirty point program for the new National Reich Church, which thankfully never came to pass with the defeat of Nazi Germany. But the plan was to confiscate all churches and chapels within Germany and any territorial frontiers of the Reich and its colonies. Nazi Party orators were to replace pastors and chaplains. Further details as follows, echo the very nature of the violent, savage Fascism of Islam (simply insert the word **Koran** for the words **Mein Kampf** below to get the full meaning):

> *"After forbidding the printing and importation of the Bible in Germany, the program calls for the National Reich Church to remove from the altars of all churches the Bible, the Cross, and other religious objects and in their place will be set that which must be venerated by the German people and therefore is by God, our most saintly book,* **Mein Kampf***, and to the left of this a sword."* [236]

---

235 <u>The Foe We Face</u> by Pierre Huss, 1942, p. 235
236 <u>Four Years of Nazi Torture</u> by Ernst Winkler, 1942, p. 197

How is it possible to corrupt the minds of children, to think and to speak of others only in terms of contempt, hatred and murder? By the constant indoctrination of hate toward others, for the express purpose of eventually carrying out violence against those that one hates.

Victor Klemperer was a learned Dresden University professor of languages. He was Jewish, and married to a German woman. Because he was married to a German, he escaped the crematorium of a concentration camp. But he suffered many deprivations, beatings and slanders during Hitler's reign. Just as Muslims teach their children hate and murder, so Nazi Germany did with their Hitler Youth groups. Here is what a group of boys said as they passed this Jewish professor on the street:

> *"At ten o'clock in the evening on Wormser Strasse, a group of boys on bicycles, fourteen to fifteen years of age. They overtake me, shout, wait, let me pass. 'He'll get a shot in the back of the head.' 'I'll pull the trigger.' 'He'll be hanged on the gallows--stock exchange racketeer' and some other muttering."* [237]

In schools, all curriculum under Hitler was "Nazified". History was falsified both by teachers and the books which they were required to use. One gets the distinct impression that mandated racial prejudice became thoroughly infused in school:

> *"The teaching of the 'racial sciences' exalting the Germans as the master race, and the Jews as breeders of almost all the evil there was in the world, was even more so."* [238]

---

237 <u>I Will Bear Witness</u> by Victor Klemperer, 1999, p. 241
238 <u>The Rise and Fall of the Third Reich</u> by William Shirer, p.250

As youth approached adulthood, Fascist Germany's raw army recruits in World War Two were young men who were not like recruits in free nations:

"He already has been through his first military teething in the Hitler Youth and the Labor Service. He is usually tough and bronzed and healthy after a year of building roads, airfields, and bridges. He has learned to march and fire a rifle and he is amenable to discipline. In fact, he already is a half-trained soldier. That was exactly how Hitler planned it should be when he set about the job of building a military machine to conquer Europe." [239]

ISLAMIC EXAMPLE OF INDOCTRINATING CHILDREN

It is common knowledge at this present time that Muslims in many countries indoctrinate their children from an early age, with a specific hatred of Jews, and Christians. Children are schooled in guerrilla warfare, the firing of rocket propelled grenades, and the use of explosives carried in vests, in which the child or young person, boy or girl, is expected to kill both their perceived enemies and their own selves by setting off the explosives in a crowd or on a bus. Israel has for years been a chief beneficiary of such violence from Muslim terrorists.

Islamic conventions are held in the United States year by year. One convention in Toledo, Ohio of the Muslim Arab Youth Association (MAYA) offered a typical mass marketing approach to

---

239 <u>This is the Enemy</u> by Frederick Oechsner, 1942, p. 191

American Muslims attending, in the sale of literature for children intended to instill hatred for Jews:

> *"A children's coloring book in Arabic featured caricatures of evil-looking, hook-nosed bearded characters emblazoned with Jewish stars."* [240]

Coloring books for children spawning racial and religious hatred toward others, is indefensible and marks Islam as Fascism because hatred, especially racial hatred, is a key element in Fascist ideology. Imagine the legal trouble anyone would have in American court rooms if such blatant racism was taught to children in American public schools!

Other books offered at the Muslim conference just described included titles like "Freemasons and Christians Conspiracy Against Islam" and "The Myth of Jesus Christ." [241] The fear that others want to harm them is a lie that Fascists promulgate, to help justify their own aggressive behavior.

Another Muslim conference featured children ages eight and nine singing songs to the praise of Hamas, the Palestinian terrorist organization, and while singing, imitating Hamas-style knife stabbings to the beat of the music. [242]

---

240 <u>American Jihad: The Terrorists Living Among Us</u> by Steven Emerson, 2002, p. 189
241 Ibid., p. 189
242 Ibid., p. 97

Schoolbooks in Egypt, Syria and Iraq in recent times taught children that Socialism was merely Islam when fully comprehended. The emphasis in Islam, as with Communism, is on the State or the nation as a whole, not on the individual.[243]

AMERICA: LOSS OF FREEDOM OF SPEECH BROUGHT DECADENCE

The Declaration of Independence states "...We hold these truths to be self-evident, that all men are created equal, that they are endowed by their Creator with certain unalienable Rights, that among these are life, liberty and the pursuit of happiness. That to secure these rights, Governments are instituted among men, deriving their just powers from the consent of the governed..."

It is the duty of patriotic Americans to press for the right of free speech, which Americans no longer have. In America today, the U.S. Supreme Court is where our national government derives its powers, not from the consent of the governed! The Court has elevated itself to the position of a godhead with its rulings. This Court of nine judges severely and effectively restricted American citizen's right to free speech, thought and religion when the reading and study of the Christian Bible and prayer were banned in the public schools.

If we Americans are forbidden to include certain subjects in schools, then we do not have freedom of speech! Communist and other Fascist nations are afraid of the Holy Bible and ban it because

---

243 <u>Jihad: The Trail of Political Islam</u> by Gilles Kepel, 2002, p. 47

they know it is life changing! Liberals hate the Bible as much as Communists do, and have decidedly changed the very character of America for the worse, via Federal court rulings which our Congress is too cowardly to redress.

American public education of children has gone astray. America was founded on religious freedoms established from Bible principles by numerous Bible believing Christian leaders, whose faith is clearly stated in America's founding documents and founder's writings. Yet ironically, the Biblical Christian faith of our fathers is the one religion currently banned from public education and discourse by our own judicial infidels!

America's roots were in the righteous, good Book that made America great. Peaceful protest with regard to exercising free speech is long overdue in America. It is necessary to overcome the limiting of free speech which became reality by judicial edict with the banning of the Bible in public schools, and indirectly its banning in public life. Free speech naturally includes the right to read and discuss any book.

The Bible and Christian prayer were included in public education in America for over two hundred years! For example, a Massachusetts law passed in 1647, established a system of public schools whose curriculum included Bible teaching and Bible memorization.

Later on in our history, in the 19th century, 122 million copies of McGuffey's Eclectic Readers were printed. There was a separate edition for each of the first six grades of primary education in the public schools, with emphasis on spelling, vocabulary, and formal public speaking. Here is an example. This one lesson--for fifth grade students--about religion and life is more profound than the ramblings of the U.S. Supreme Court regarding religion:

> *"Religion is a social concern...Erase all thought and fear of God from a community, and selfishness and sensuality would absorb the whole man. Appetite, knowing no restraint, and suffering, having no solace or hope, would trample in scorn on the restraints of human laws. Virtue, duty, principle, would be mocked and spurned as unmeaning sounds. A sordid self-interest would supplant every feeling; and man would become, in fact, what the theory in atheism declares him to be--a companion for brutes."* [244]

McGuffey's Eclectic Readers contained excerpts from the Bible, from America's great founders, and from works of well-regarded English and American writers. John Milton's works were included, a writer whose prose and poetry involved a passion for freedom and self-determination. McGuffey's Reader lessons such as "Beware of the First Drink" taught young people right from wrong. [245] Find a public school that would include that particular short story against beverage alcohol in their readings today!

Since the Bible and prayer were banned from America's public schools in 1962-1963 by the U.S. Supreme Court, Bible principles once taught to children in school are disappearing if not already gone. What principles? These would include things like common

---

244 <u>McGuffey's Fifth Eclectic Reader</u>, Revised Edition, undated, pp. 285-286
245 Ibid., p. 111

courtesy, respect for elders, diligence, hard work, self-government, self-reliance, and moral purity just to name a few.

The Bible book of Proverbs teaches young people to seek wisdom, to avoid bad friendships, to abstain from the evils of strong drink, and many other important character traits. Sex education classes were not necessary in bygone days in America, because young people were taught the plain fact that sexual intimacy was for marriage only, and young people in mixed company were chaperoned as is proper and necessary.

In 1960, which is just before America caved into the loss of our First Amendment rights to free speech by the banning of the Bible from the public schools, only 5% of babies were born to unwed mothers in the United States. In 2013, 41% of all babies born in the U.S.A. were born to mothers outside of marriage.[246] America no longer has a moral compass, or THE moral compass of the Holy Bible to guide families.

Sadly each generation that comes along defines what is socially acceptable, which has become less and less virtuous. Ironically, Islam, with its well-known polygamous ways, descries the moral decadence of America in recitations of hatred. Rather like the pot calling the kettle black.

America defended the defenseless in two World Wars, and rebuilt Europe afterward at our expense, out of Christian duty. Between 1947-1952, the U.S. Congress appropriated $13 billion to rebuild western Europe after World War Two under the Marshall

---

246 http://www.childtrends.org/?indicators=births-to-unmarried-women

Plan.[247] America used to be a place where children were taught the golden rule, that is, to do unto others as they would have them to do unto themselves. But without the Bible as its guide, America has produced more criminal activity, a drug culture, a welfare mentality, many children born from unwed parents, and millions of unborn babies legally murdered by abortion.

President Dwight Eisenhower, in 1955, had a very astute vision of the future of American public education when he wrote:

> *"To give Washington the responsibility for the perpetual support of the educational function would, I was convinced, ultimately bring on federal control of education...Even a nationalized curriculum might eventually ensue if the trend line of federal aid to education permanently went up. The final result would be the loss of true academic freedom and variety in education."*[248]

This is exactly what has happened to American public school education. The U.S. Department of Education in Washington D.C. influences curriculum in the public schools of America today. The control originates from Congressional laws, rules and guidelines which must be met in order to receive Federal dollars to operate the public schools. Washington, of course, seldom gives away money unless certain requirements are met.

America prior to the 1960's, was a nation of people not afraid of plain truth. President Dwight Eisenhower, for example, advocated

---

247 The Aftermath Europe by Douglas Botting, 1983, p. 154
248 Mandate for Change by Dwight D. Eisenhower, 1963, p. 500

that the public schools should include teaching students about how difficult life was under Russian communism, so that they would have a better appreciation of American freedoms. Truth imparts wisdom and discretion.

Children need to learn what our freedoms are, and the source from which they are derived. It is said that today's soldiers do not really understand what it is the United States stands for, or what it is that they are expected to defend in battle. The reason today's soldiers don't know what America stands for, is because they are no longer taught about the difference between life in a free country versus life under Communism. Such confusion extends all the way up to and including our nation's elected officials.

Tablet computers and "smart phones" are replacing books in schools. Teaching America's distinctly Christian history is minimized, and replaced with teaching about diversity and multiculturalism. Has learning declined? Scores on college entrance exams have declined to the point where such tests have been re-written and changed in structure and length, in order that current scores cannot be readily compared with the better scores attained in scholastic tests from years gone by.

Home skills are no longer emphasized in America's public schools, to the detriment of home and family. In bygone days, every girl was taught to sew a dress or skirt in a home economics class. That old fashioned learning has been replaced with girls on sports teams, in immodest apparel. The majority of high school girls graduating today know little or nothing of how to sew their own clothing, which is a worthwhile enterprise for a future wife and mother of children.

Do not forget that the loss of freedom of speech plays into the hands of tyrants, whether they be Socialists, Communists, or Fascists.

The meeting opened with twelve hundred brown-shirted Nazi's in tall jackboots marching by drumbeat into the crowded arena, with Nazi swastika flags.[251] The enemies of patriotic, white Americans, it was pronounced, were Jews, negroes, Communists, labor unions, Catholics, and democracy itself. One speaker stated the laughable idea that Jews had picked the current Pope, and that Jews held a $15 million mortgage on the Vatican itself. The attendees, in general, could best be described as the uninformed.

What sort of people were in attendance at meetings such as this in New York? There were people in ignorance or in willing ignorance of the events taking place in western Europe and elsewhere. There were others in attendance who did not look beneath the titles of the sponsoring organizations.

The right-sounding American Patriots, Inc. was in fact a sister organization of the American National Socialist Party. This group held luncheons at upscale hotels in large American cities to propagandize Americans and to raise money. The name of many of these organizations belied what they represented. "The crowd was distinctly Park Avenue, composed mostly of women wearing dresses fashionable a decade ago; bloodless, bitter old dowagers looking for political excitement and willing to pay for it."[252]

Here in the United States, just prior to and during World War Two, scare tactics were used by a former radio station

---

251 <u>Under Cover</u> by John Roy Carlson, 1943, p. 26
252 Ibid., p. 48

announcer named Allen Zoll who spoke of making America safe from a Communist revolution. He told the women at an American Patriots group meeting, "Do you realize what it will mean to have 13 million Communist niggers turned loose? Need I tell you what happened to Hungarian peasant girls?"[253]

There was hatred and violence toward Jews, Democrats, Republicans, and anyone else that stood in the way of strong arm tactics. Ruffians in these National Socialist organizations marched through the streets of New York, Chicago and other cities anxious to fight anyone who dared criticize their banners and pamphlets. Steel pipes wrapped in newspapers, and brass knuckles were part of every march and demonstration.

After the armed Nazi invasion of Poland in September, 1939, a crowd of 2,000 people gathered in New York with the American Nationalist Party to sing German folk songs. Then a film of the invasion of Poland by Germany was shown. "A bomb heaved from an airplane laid waste an area teeming with life. The audience went into hysterics."[254]

This same phenomenon, that of ignoring immense human suffering at the hands of evil men is alive and well in America today. For while militant Islam is daily going about its global business of murdering the innocent, and making war against non-Muslims, there are white and black skinned Americans in the United States identifying themselves as "converted" Muslims.

---

253 <u>Under Cover</u> by John Roy Carlson, 1943, p. 49
254 Ibid., p. 440

These people have believed the lie that Islam is a religion of peace! Impossible, one would think, that Americans could be hoodwinked into believing that Islam is a religion of peace, while Muslim leaders in the Mideast and elsewhere shout the cry of "death to America" and violent acts against innocent civilians continue unabated.

Almost daily the news is tainted with reports of Islamic-inspired bloodshed from somewhere in the world. But again, willing ignorance is widely exhibited toward the violent nature of Islamic Fascism. As it was in Germany seventy years ago, so it is with Islam today.

Fascism is alive and well right here in America. Clandestine organizations are at work, without violence, to undermine freedom in America by putting Americans to sleep to the dangers involved in accepting the tenets of Islam, which is a political ideology, not a religion. Make no mistake about it.

What will the final cost be to America in combating Islam if it is not declared to be the enemy of America and of freedom and actions taken to contain its influence and activities? The cost may well be more than sending American troops and money around the globe to fight Islamic terrorism as we now do. But it may eventually result in open, armed combat with Muslim forces right here on American soil.

Wake up America! Islam has declared war on us. Don't we all know that by now? America must declare war on Islam, the first step of which is to admit that Islam is not a religion but a savage political ideology of death or subjugation of its opponents.

German citizens succumbed in fear to the violent nature and the lies of Nazi Fascism for twelve years, and lived to regret it. It was nearly six years from the date of the Nazi invasion of Poland on September 1, 1939, until Germany was defeated in World War Two as the opposing Allied forces took action. Germany surrendered unconditionally to American forces on May 7, 1945 ending the Second World War in Europe. Official Victory in Europe (VE Day) was celebrated the next day, May 8th, 1945.

The final cost of Nazi aggression against other nations is glaringly apparent in Germany itself after World War Two. As an occupied country, the victor's Allied Council took a census of the population of Germany in 1946, one year after the war ended. It determined that the proportion of women to men ages 20-30 in Germany was in a ratio of 15 to 1, a high cost to the German people for their naked aggression. This brought about, among other things, a huge labor shortage for agriculture, industry and the rebuilding of Germany. Due to this shortage, no railroad locomotives, crucial in transport of food and in rebuilding Germany itself, were expected to be built there until 1949.[255]

The cost to America could be much more than several thousand lives and a couple of skyscrapers destroyed if we do not awake to the threat of Islam.

---

255 <u>Coast Artillery Journal</u>, May-June, 1946, p. 60-61

CHAPTER 14

Fascists are liars
(their actions speak louder)

———

THE EXAMPLE OF NAZI FASCIST LIES

SO, WHAT IS THERE TO worry about? Much, because Fascists cannot be taken at their word. Hitler became German Chancellor on January 30, 1933. Hitler lied. He arranged a fire in the Reichstag (legislature's) building, then requested unlimited, emergency powers from Germany's legislative branch to deal with a supposed attempt to take over the government by Communists who he blamed for the fire.

Then, through imprisoning many elected politicians and making threats to others, he secured for himself permanent, unlimited powers as German Chancellor without any restrictions on his authority. Hitler's reign of terror lasted for twelve bloody years. The thing to remember is, that while Fascists speak peace, lies, violence and murder is on their minds.

On September 5, 1934, Adolf Hitler gave a rousing speech to thirty thousand of his automaton followers in Luitpold Hall at Nuremberg, Germany. Amidst his address, he proclaimed: "Germany has done everything possible to assure world peace. If war comes to Europe, it will come only because of Communist chaos."[256] This was quite a blatant lie, considering the warfare Germany subsequently initiated throughout Europe under his leadership.

In Berlin, on March 17, 1935, Hitler gave his Heroes Memorial Day speech to commemorate the two million Germans who died in World War One. To France he gave his promise of peace in the speech:

> *"Germany has finally given France the solemn assurance that Germany, after the adjustment of the Saar question, now no longer will make territorial demands upon France."* [257]

To Germans and to the world, in the same speech, he said:

> *In this hour the German government renews before the German people and before the entire world its assurance of its determination never to proceed beyond the safeguarding of German honour and the freedom of the Reich, and especially it does not intend in rearming Germany to create any instrument for warlike attack, but, on the contrary, exclusively for defense and thereby for the maintenance of peace. In so doing, the Reich government expresses the confident hope that the German people, having again obtained their*

---

256 <u>Berlin Diary</u> by William Shirer, 1941, pp. 18-19
257 Ibid., p. 34

own honour, may be privileged in independent equality to make their contribution towards the pacification of the world in free and open co-operation with other nations." [258]

Two months later, on May 21, 1935, Hitler gave another Berlin speech in the Reichstag, the German national parliament, regarding peace which included these remarks:

"...Germany needs peace...Germany wants peace...No one of us means to threaten anybody..." [259]

In the same speech, Hitler launched into a thirteen point program for Germany's future which included, he claimed, Germany's desire to abolish the heaviest armaments including heavy artillery and heavy tanks, to outlaw the dropping of gas, incendiary and explosive bombs on non-military targets in war, specifically those areas where damage and death would affect civilian populations. He suggested that even the complete prohibition of submarines by all nations might be agreeable to Germany. [260]

On March 7, 1936, Hitler spoke on war and peace. It was his way of negotiating with foreign powers, a logical and lasting peace proposal. In it, "Hitler offers to sign a twenty-five year non-aggression pact with Belgium and France..." [261]

---

258 <u>Berlin Diary</u> by William Shirer, 1941, p. 34.
259 Ibid., p. 37
260 Ibid., p. 39
261 <u>Berlin Diary</u> by William Shirer, 1941, p. 51

However, actions speak louder than words. Hitler's actions in the years that followed his taking absolute power in Germany in 1933, were true to his desires as expressed in his book <u>Mein Kampf</u> (My Struggle). Here is a quote from the book, as translated into English by William Shirer:

> *"France is to be annihilated, says Hitler, and then the great drive to the eastward is to begin."* [262]

Here are the headlines of a Berlin Nazi newspaper, the Volkische Beobachter (meaning Folk Observer) on October 8, 1939, disseminating Adolf Hitler's spoken intentions for Germany:

> *"Germany's Will for Peace--No War Aims Against France--No More Revision Claims Except Colonies--Reduction of Armaments--Co-Operation with All Nations of Europe--Proposal for a Conference"* [263]

What followed in the ensuing years? (Austria had already been occupied by German armies and Poland invaded). Total war was to follow. It was all lies. More than a year earlier, in a parade in Berlin, on August 25, 1938, goose-stepping Nazi Army troops marched along before huge field guns with eleven inch bore, larger than any field guns in existence other than full-size battleships. Enormous new heavy tanks were also exhibited in this parade as Germany began to let its massive buildup of arms be shown to the world, a prelude to war. This was Hitler's real intention for the future.

---

262 Ibid., p. 86
263 Ibid., pp. 232-233

Germans were told by the Nazis that the country needed li-ebensraum, which means living space. That too was a lie. The population density of Germany in 1937 was 362 people per square mile, while the population per square mile of other countries was as follows: Belgium, 707 people; Holland 673 people; and England 488 people per square mile.[264]

What happened when Hitler invaded other nations? Martial law was declared, meaning all civil rights thereby ended. All food and natural resources were overseen and commandeered. Borders were closed. Government officials and police were replaced. Universities were closed. All unions and political parties were banned. Ration cards were issued for food purchases. Impromptu Gestapo house inspections were immediately begun. Arrests and executions started. All newspapers and other media were placed under Nazi control. Those are the kinds of events and transforma-tions that Fascism brings!

Here is a chronological listing of unprovoked, naked, military aggression by Hitler's Fascist German empire, in which other na-tions were attacked and occupied by German armed forces:

October 15, 1938 - German troops occupy the Sudetenland, part of Czechoslavakia. The Czech government resigns.

March 15, 1939 - German troops march in to take the entire country of Czechoslavakia, with six years of enslavement under the heel of Nazi oppression and mass murder to follow. The actions of

---

264 <u>Time Runs Out</u> by Henry J. Taylor, 1942, p. 30

the Nazis was contrary to their lies of peace to all. The previous September, Nazi Herman Goering said of the Czechs:

> "...*This miserable pygmy race (the Czechs) without culture--no one knows where it came from--is oppressing a cultured people and behind it is Moscow and the eternal mask of the Jew devil...* "[265]

September 1, 1939 - German air force and armies invade Poland in massive warfare after staging a fake attack on Germany by Poland using German prisoners in Polish Army uniforms. Poland is subsequently divided into two territories, split in half with the east taken over by Russia, the west half taken as German territory.

April 9, 1940 - Germany invades Denmark and Norway with the stated intention of protecting them from attack by England. This invasion of both countries involves German bombing, occupation, lootings, jailings, deportations and enslavement.

An example of how Germany cared for their protectorates is seen in the speech given in Oslo, Norway by Herr Terboven, Reich Commissar of occupied Norway, on October 4, 1941, concerning the food shortage in Norway:

> "*It is a matter of indifference to Germany whether some thousands or tens of thousands of Norwegian men, women and children starve and freeze to death during this war.*" [266]

---

265 <u>Berlin Diary</u> by William Shirer, 1941, p. 126
266 <u>Underground Europe</u> by Curt Riess, 1942, p. 128

May 10, 1940 - Germany invades France, Belgium, Luxembourg, and the Netherlands (Holland). Once again, civilians are murdered by the thousands in their homes, offices, or even in their cars or on foot while fleeing German bombers and strafing fighter planes. 78,000 are made homeless from the initial bombing raids of Amsterdam, Holland alone.[267]

> *"The Dutch could not collaborate with those who had invaded their country without warning. They could not forget how German bombers had appeared over Holland without a previous declaration of war. First they had been showered with Nazi leaflets claiming that the country needed German protection against the French and the British; then bombs laid waste large parts of their cities. The Dutch could not forget the ruins of Rotterdam."* [268]

All of these western European countries came under Nazi domination and virtual enslavement, with arrest, torture and death for many who were Jews, or who opposed the Fascists or refused to help produce German munitions. The enslavement lasted over five years, until Allied armies invaded the continent of Europe on June 6, 1944, and attained victory over Fascist Germany. Unconditional surrender of Germany was marked on May 7, 1945. (A surrender ceremony was repeated in Berlin the next day to satisfy the Russians.)

September 7, 1940 - Germany begins the bombing of England, including massive air raids on civilian areas of London, Bristol, Southampton, Liverpool and Manchester. (In one attack alone

---

267 <u>The Rise and Fall of the Third Reich</u> by William Shirer, 1960, p.722
268 <u>Underground Europe</u> by Curt Riess, 1942, p. 100

at Birmingham, almost eight hundred people are killed and two thousand injured.) Mass graves for bomb victims are common, especially in London, a city of seven million people. Bombing raids last for 73 nights in succession.[269]

Yet Hitler's minions broadcast pure lies over the radio to German citizens about the conduct of their savage bombings:

"While the attack of the German air force is made on purely military objectives--this fact is recognized by both the British press and radio--the R.A.F. knows nothing better to do than continually to attack non-military objectives in Germany. A perfect example of this was the criminal attack on the middle of Berlin last night. In this attack only lodging houses were hit; not a single military objective."[270]

The truth was that in August, 1940 alone, more than one thousand English civilians were killed by bombs, contrary to Germany's claim that they only bombed military targets.[271]

October 7, 1940 - Germany attacks Romania and brings the whole country under Nazi rule.

February 14, 1941 - Germany's Afrika Corps army arrives in Tunisia, to fight and retake Libya which Italian armies have lost to English armies, and to attempt to drive on eastward to seize Egypt, the Suez Canal and middle east oil fields.

---

269 Their Finest Hour by Winston Churchill, 1949, p. 342
270 Berlin Diary by William Shirer, 1941, p. 499-500
271 Berlin Diary by William Shirer, 1941, p. 500

April 6, 1941 - German army and air force invade Greece and Yugoslavia with heavy civilian casualties.

June 22, 1941 - Germany's armed forces attack the Soviet Union. Death squads follow the German onslaught, murdering literally millions of Soviet Jews and partisans. (Nazis murder over 30,000 Jews at the city of Kiev alone.) Nearly four years of barbaric warfare are to follow before the defeat of Germany.

December 11, 1941 - Germany declares war on the United States. Unrestricted submarine warfare against American military and commercial vessels begins, resulting in the loss of thousands of ships and merchant marine sailors. The German U-boat fleet is finally defeated in the Atlantic Ocean in May, 1943 through the efforts of joint American and British navy and air force anti-submarine warfare.

June 13, 1944 - The first unmanned flying bombs/rockets hit England. Over 9,500 of these bombs devastate England, killing more than 6,000 people, seriously injuring over 18,000 and causing untold millions of dollars in property damage.[272]

There is an old saying that if a lie is repeated often enough, it will eventually be believed as truth. How deeply imbedded lies can become, even in the face of reality. Lies that cause people not to believe that they themselves were lied to, resulting in a total inability to accept blame for the tragic crimes and results of war!

---

272 The History Place, World War Two in Europe, Timeline, www.thehistoryplace.com

A report of an interview with the mayor of a German town after the total defeat and surrender of Nazi Germany in 1945 reads as follows:

"The mayor, like so many others, nevertheless, said he thought Hitler was a 'good man' who had Germany's interest at heart. Hitler had done the best he could, trying to help Germany against the attacks by Russia, England, and the United States."[273]

Fascist followers, like their masters, also lie and cannot believe the truth. The great Krupp armament works in Essen, Germany, made artillery pieces, armor plate, bombs and hulls for tanks for Hitler's armies in World War Two. In another post-war interview in Germany, the Managing Director of Krupp, stated that Krupp only made what the government ordered. He further attested that if Essen had not been bombed 28 times by the Allies, then the 50,000 workers at Krupp would not be out of work. Here was his mentality:

"This concern', Herr Houdremont insisted, with a note of irritability in his voice, 'was never controlled by the Nazis. It was a private concern. Krupp's made only what the German government ordered, no more, no less, and how can the Allies expect a peaceful Europe after they have bombed such great plants out of existence...Perhaps we will need loans from America to build up Krupp's again' he said."[274]

---

273 <u>Men and Power</u> by Henry J. Taylor, 1946, p. 190
274 Ibid. p. 188

This managing Director also stated in the same post-war interview that Krupp could begin to make farm machinery again as soon as possible, though the company had <u>never</u> manufactured farm machinery ever in its long history!

The refusal to accept responsibility for destructive behavior, or to feel guilt about wrongdoing, goes hand in hand with Fascist tyranny. It's not our fault, they insist, we were forced by our enemies to do what we did! This is why Fascism (under any banner) must be dealt with directly and destroyed. Winston Churchill, former Prime Minister of England, recognized and warned of the danger of Fascism:

> *"Nazi tyranny and Prussian militarism are the two main elements in German life which must be absolutely destroyed. They must be rooted out if Europe and the world are to be spared a third and still more frightful conflict."* [275]

> *"We do not war primarily with races as such. Tyranny is our foe. Whatever trapping or disguise it wears, whatever language it speaks, be it external or internal, we must forever be on our guard, ever mobilized, ever vigilant, always ready to spring at its throat. In all this we march together. Not only do we march and strive shoulder to shoulder at this moment, under the fire of the enemy on the fields of war or in the air, but also in those realms of thought which are consecrated to the rights and the dignity of man."* [276]

---

275 <u>Closing the Ring</u> by Winston Churchill, 1951, p. 159
276 Ibid., p. 124

Nazi Fascists, we must remember, not only lied about their intentions toward other nations to make war, but also carried out clandestine warfare against many of their own citizens. Starting with the boycotting of Jewish businesses, Hitler soon turned up the heat on the entire Jewish population. He banned them from professional occupations, revoked their civil rights, confiscated their homes and property, and finally, arrested the Jews, shipping them off like cattle to be worked to death or murdered outright. Even the sick and the disabled were euthanized secretly under Hitler's reign, beginning in October, 1939.

Let it not be said that the Allies in World War Two, also indiscriminately bombed German cities extensively and killed many civilians in the process. The Allies did not initiate the war, and extreme measures on the part of Allies were necessary to demoralize and defeat the warring German nation, and eliminate Nazism from the planet.

The fact that violence and war are a natural by-product of Fascist thought, can be seen in the world today via Muslim terrorists. This violence must be stopped.

If Islamic ideology can carry out its worship of its god in peace without injury or death to others, then let it co-exist in the world. If not, then all those elements and forces which represent themselves as Islamic, while demonstrating and conducting Fascist behavior (violence, war, and revolution) must be eliminated completely just as Fascist Nazism had to be eliminated.

WHY?
BECAUSE ISLAMISTS (MOSLEMS)
ARE ALSO BOLD LIARS

Islamist rulers feign Mohammedanism as a peaceful religion. But by their actions, they brook no opposition to their open hatred and active warring against non-Muslims worldwide. This violence, justified by their belief system, is held in abeyance to a large degree in developed nations where free peoples are the rule, rather than the exception. A gullability award has to go to the United States of America for negotiating in any fashion with nations or groups that sponsor, spawn, espouse or house militant Islamists or Muslim terrorists, just as America is doing at present. A treaty with Iran regarding nuclear capabilities is just one example of our naivete.

Islamic militarism and terrorism throughout the world categorically void the very thought that Islam was, is or ever could be a religion of peace. Nor are Islamic aims and plans a secret. On March 3, 2015, Israeli Prime Minister Benjamin Netanyahu spoke to a joint session of the United States Congress. His speech centered on the foolish, liberal terms the United States was proposing to negotiate with the country of Iran, in the matter of refining uranium toward the development of nuclear bomb capability.

In his speech, he stated the problem as being one of allowing a rogue, terrorist Muslim nation to be capable of destroying Israel and other nations:

"To understand just how dangerous Iran would be with nuclear weapons, we must fully understand the nature of the regime... Iran's founding document pledges death, tyranny, and the pursuit of jihad. And as states are collapsing across the Middle East, Iran is charging into the void to do just that. Iran's goons in Gaza, its lackeys in Lebanon, its revolutionary guards on the Golan Heights are clutching Israel with three tentacles of terror. Backed by Iran, Assad is slaughtering Syrians. Backed by Iran, Shiite (Muslim) militias are rampaging through Iraq. Backed by Iran, Houthis are seizing control of Yemen, threatening the strategic straits at the mouth of the Red Sea. Along with the Straits of Hormuz, that would give Iran a second choke-point on the world's oil supply.

Just last week, near Hormuz, Iran carried out a military exercise blowing up a mock U.S. aircraft carrier. That's just last week, while they're having nuclear talks with the United States." [277]

The truth here is the same as with Hitler's Fascism. While Iran feigns honest nuclear negotiations in Switzerland with gullible American governmental leaders--led by Secretary of State John Kerry--they are simultaneously practicing making warfare back home.

Netanyahu pointed out in his speech to the U.S. Congress that, for more than thirty years, the Islamic country of Iran has committed terrorist acts against the United States. For instance, he listed the Iran hostage crisis at the American Embassy in Tehran, the murder of hundreds of U.S. Marines in Beirut, Lebanon, by truck bombing

---

[277] Israel Prime Minister Benjamin Netanyahu Speech to U.S. Congress, March 3, 2015

and the war deaths of American military personnel in combat in Iraq and Afghanistan. Furthermore, Netanyahu mentioned the activities of Iran's worldwide terrorist network, which bombed a Jewish community center and the Israeli embassy in Argentina, as well as assisting Al Qaida terrorists in bombing U.S. embassies in Africa.

In the Middle East, Iran now prevails in four Arab capitals: Baghdad, Iraq; Damascus, Syria; Beirut, Lebanon; and Sanaa, Yemen. The battle is for Muslim control of the entire world. Terror-inspired Iran alone consists of 80 million Muslims, only one of many militant Islamic countries. Prime Minister Netanyahu proclaimed:

> *"Iran's regime is as radical as ever, it cries of "Death to America," that same America that it calls the "Great Satan," as loud as ever. Now, this shouldn't be surprising, because the ideology of Iran's revolutionary regime is deeply rooted in militant Islam, and that's why this regime will always be an enemy of America. Don't be fooled. The battle between Iran and ISIS doesn't turn Iran into a friend of America. Iran and ISIS are competing for the crown of militant Islam. One calls itself the Islamic Republic. The other calls itself the Islamic State. Both want to impose a militant Islamic empire first on the region and then on the entire world. They just disagree among themselves who will be the ruler of that empire. In this deadly game of thrones, there's no place for America or for Israel, no peace for Christians, Jews or Muslims who don't share the Islamist medieval creed, no rights for women, no freedom for anyone."* [278]

---

278 Israel Prime Minister Benjamin Netanyahu Speech to U.S. Congress, March 3, 2015

We understand that Iran is called the Islamic Republic. But who, as in Netanyahu's speech, is the "Islamic State?" It is none other than a separate, Islamic terrorist group intent on world domination with their own brand of Islam. The full name of these Islamic terrorists is "Islamic State in Iraq and Ash-Sham" or better known in the English speaking world as "ISIS."[279]

In regard to how these two Islamic forces for evil relate to free peoples, Netanyahu stated "the enemy of your enemy is your enemy."[280] In other words, both the Islamic terrorist regime of Iran **and** the ISIS band of terrorists are the enemy of free peoples. Netanyahu said further:

> *"The difference is that ISIS is armed with butcher knives, captured weapons and YouTube, whereas Iran could soon be armed with intercontinental ballistic missiles and nuclear bombs. We must always remember -- I'll say it one more time -- the greatest dangers facing our world is the marriage of militant Islam with nuclear weapons. To defeat ISIS and let Iran get nuclear weapons would be to win the battle, but lose the war."* [281]

Mr. Netanyahu's speech in Washington, D.C. on March 3, 2015 was a plea for leaders of the free world to wake up to reality. Unfortunately, American politicians were not listening. Things are not getting better, they are deteriorating.

---

279 What is ISIS?, Article by David Stansfield, www.infowars.com
280 Israel Prime Minister Benjamin Netanyahu Speech to U.S. Congress, March 3, 2015
281 Israel Prime Minister Benjamin Netanyahu Speech to U.S. Congress, March 3, 2015

Consider the similarity of Mr. Netanyahu's 2015 speech given at the United Nations nearly five years earlier (2010):

> *" This Iranian regime is fueled by an extreme fundamentalism that burst onto the world scene three decades ago after lying dormant for centuries. In the past thirty years, this fanaticism has swept the globe with a murderous violence and cold-blooded impartiality in its choice of victims. It has callously slaughtered Moslems and Christians, Jews and Hindus, and many others. Though it is comprised of different offshoots, the adherents of this unforgiving creed seek to return humanity to medieval times.*
>
> *Wherever they can, they impose a backward regimented society where women, minorities, gays or anyone not deemed to be a true believer is brutally subjugated. The struggle against this fanaticism does not pit faith against faith nor civilization against civilization.*
>
> *It pits civilization against barbarism, the 21st century against the 9th century, those who sanctify life against those who glorify death."* [282]

The free world must face the fact that today we have in existence not only openly murderous Islamic regimes such as Iran that would wipe out Israel and America and other free peoples, but there are Islamic terrorist organizations at war now that compete for the lead part in the destruction! ISIS is only one relatively new player. There is also Boko Haram, Al Qaida, Hamas, Hezbollah, Islamic Jihad, Muslim Brotherhood, and others.

---

282 Israel Prime Minister Benjamin Netanyahu Speech to the United Nations General Assembly, September 24, 2010, New York, NY

What Muslims say can also be easily doubted because lying and deceiving is not forbidden in the Koran. This lying is spelled out in the Koran as keeping circumstances under one's control when working with so-called unbelievers. The Koran states not to accept unbelievers as friends "except when taking precaution against them in prudence." (Koran 3:28) This is widely interrupted within Islam to mean that it is perfectly all right to lie to non-Muslims.[283]

The Bill of Rights of the United States Constitution guarantees the free exercise of religion. However, such free exercise, in the mind of any sane individual, does not include:

* decapitation of one's enemies;
* the hijacking and kamikaze crashing of airplanes into buildings;
* the murder by gunfire or bombing of innocent civilians;
* the kidnapping and enslavement of females as sex slaves.

All of the above are known by-products of the "religion" of Islam, and must be fought against and conquered for the peaceful continuance of the human race.

---

283 The Complete Infidel's Guide to ISIS by Robert Spencer, 2015, pp. 59-60

CHAPTER 15

Why Fascist ideologies Do Not Last

———

THERE ARE A NUMBER OF reasons why Fascist ideologies come to an end. One principal reason historically is that the power of the governmental authority which backs up the Fascism is lost. An example would be the Roman Catholic church, which with the breakup of the Roman empire no longer had the authority to make violent conquests against its enemies. Separation of church--or any religion--from the power and authority of government is a positive step for freedom of thought, speech and doctrinal beliefs.

Russian Communism is a Fascist system that still exists today, but has lost a fair degree of its power due to economic collapse of the Soviet Union. A number of former provinces and states have declared their independence from Russia in the past twenty years or so. As a consequence much capital has come into those new sovereign countries. And now, Russia would have them back in the fold again, for obvious reasons. The Ukraine, breadbasket of eastern Europe, would certainly head the list for Russian subjugation by military force.

The Ukraine's trouble is an ongoing battle. Remember, Fascists attack and try to take what they want by force. Kazikstan could also be up for grabs in the near future, now that billions of dollars have been poured into the development of crude oil production in that country.

Unfortunately for human beings, Fascism under Hitler had to run a twelve year bloody course, requiring the armed forces of most of the free world to be engaged in delivering many captive nations from the grip of the Nazis. The Second World War itself encompassed six years and resulted in the deaths of about 72 million people. Just 11 million of that number were those of the Axis powers--the Fascists of Japan, Germany and Italy that started the war. The remaining 61 million people were innocents killed before the tyrants were stopped. Included in the 61 million were 22 million soldiers, and all the rest, 39 million people, were civilians including 6 million Jews slaughtered or starved to death.[284]

Fascism does not go away in and of itself. It is either defeated militarily, or changes in political structure/climate bring about its demise. Nazism did not hide its evil intents for very long before its violent and destructive character was identified as an enemy of all free people. Islamic violence is likewise carried on in the world today, but the ill-bred doctrines of multi-culturalism, diversity, and favoritism of minority religions and causes blinds our leaders from calling Islam what it is--Fascism.

---

284 www.http:www2.org/uk

THE POWER OF TRUTH

In Europe in World War Two, there were about 300 million people under the Nazi yoke. All press and news was censored and controlled by Germany. The truth about how battles were going was altered, and the truth about Nazi oppression, executions, starvation and so on were not told to the masses. The exception was the British Broadcasting Corporation or BBC:

"In a sense, the British Broadcasting Corporation or BBC, was Europe's last stronghold of freedom and truth. Almost the whole continent lay fettered under the heel of the dictator. The news reports originating on the continent were issued by the conqueror. People had to take Hitler's word. Under the circumstances, this last fortress that could withstand the campaign of outright lies and twisted fact had to be held. Too many of Hitler's conquests had been prepared for by a systematic spreading of false reports." [285]

"Clearly there was still a country left that dared to defy Hitler. Truth still had a refuge in Europe. To be the final refuge of embattled truth, was a great responsibility. The BBC recognized and accepted this responsibility. Never, not for a day, not for an hour did it yield to the passions of war and embittered partisanship to the extent of lowering its standards of reliable reporting. The BBC knew that lies could be fought only by those who would not lie." [286]

---

285 <u>Underground Europe</u> by Curt Riess, 1942, p. 172
286 <u>Underground Europe</u> by Curt Riess, 1942, p. 173

As the Czechoslovakian author Milan Kundera wrote about the quest for freedom from tyranny and lies, "The struggle of man against power is the struggle of memory against forgetting."[287]

The BBC had thousands of workers for its short wave radio broadcasts. They sent out nearly eighty news bulletins to western Europe each day totaling over 300,000 words.[288] Each occupied country came to know at what time they could hear a fifteen minute summary of news in their own language.

There was a central desk for each occupied country in the BBC offices, where dozens of people brought news reports that were gathered and sifted for broadcast. These incoming reports came from secret shortwave encoded Morse code radio broadcasts received from underground forces or Allied spies in the occupied countries.

The BBC effort went on around the clock. It was part of the offensive battle against Nazi Fascism, bringing truth to the millions of people who had no way of knowing how the war was progressing. Berlin propaganda-style news always had the Nazi's winning, which was more and more often a lie after the North African battle of Alamein in November of 1942.

The Nazis imposed stiff prison sentences or even summary execution for those caught listening to the BBC both in Germany and in all occupied countries.[289] Fascists want their unhappy followers to hear only what they want them to hear.

---

287 The Black Book of the American Left by D Horowitz, 2013, p.177
288 Underground Europe by Curt Riess, 1942, p. 194
289 Berlin Diary by William Shirer, 1941, p. 262

Radios were ordered to be surrendered to authorities in some occupied countries. The shortage or absence of radios led to the British dropping small radio sets by the thousands into Poland and elsewhere by parachute.[290] Clandestine radio listening became a watchful art. People wanted to know the truth!

Underground forces developed stronger and stronger throughout Europe during the Second World War. The Allies dropped arms and supplies to these secret armies who conducted sabotage against the German Nazis. Much of their efforts were aided and coordinated by signals given out on BBC radio broadcasts. The signals were coded words which were meaningless to the Nazis but triggered planned activity by underground forces. "The green worm is in the closet" and "Marie loves her pink umbrella" are two examples of such coded messages, read by BBC radio announcers at random times during the middle of other country-specific news material.[291]

The BBC shortwave radio broadcasts, once heard, were also disseminated by underground forces in Europe. The news, either written by hand or typeset, was then distributed to the people, often nothing more than mimeograph sheets. Good news from a far country is likened, in an old saying, to a drink of cold water to a thirsty soul.

Thus, the BBC was also a great encouragement to those who did not have radios as well as those who did not want to risk arrest

---

290 <u>Underground Europe</u> by Curt Riess, 1942, p. 196
291 <u>Journey Underground</u> by David G. Prosser, 1945, p. 234

and imprisonment, even death, for listening to the BBC news broadcasts. Britain is to be commended for all that the nation of just forty million people did to help win the war against Hitler's Germany.

Truth was also used to discourage the enemies. Via short wave radio, the BBC sent news to the Germans themselves. Daily broadcasts into Germany gave the names 'and hometowns of all Nazi armed forces who had been captured by the Allies. The names of German soldiers who had been killed in battle were also broadcast, if their identity could be ascertained. Though forbidden to listen, Germans listened aptly, hoping not to hear the name(s) of their own family or acquaintances.

What people groups on this planet are allowed to conduct their own lives in accordance with their own wishes? Is it not free people, that are free from the threat of incarceration or death for how they speak, or live, or vote in an election? Winston Churchill was compelled to give a speech in the House of Parliament on December 8, 1944 to put democracy in its proper perspective. The speech was necessitated because of political forces manifested in the news media of London. The news media opposed and misrepresented his actions. Churchill was trying to help the nation of Greece avoid being hostage to a new group of Communist barbarians who were poised to take over the country when the Nazis were driven out.

So while the BBC broadcast truth to the Nazi occupied countries, the news media at home in Britain was disseminating untruths about the actions of Churchill's government and armed forces, who were set about to help prevent anarchy and Communism from enslaving Greece. He said:

> *"I say that the last thing that represents democracy is mob law and the attempt to introduce a totalitarian regime which clamors to shoot everyone who is politically inconvenient as part of a purge of those who are said to have collaborated with the Germans during the occupation. Do not rate democracy so low, do not let us rate democracy as if it were merely grabbing power and shooting those who do not agree with you. That is the antithesis of democracy. Democracy is not based on violence or terrorism, but on reason, on fair play, on freedom, on respecting the rights of other people. Democracy is no harlot to be picked up in the street by a man with a tommy gun."* [292]

CHOOSING FREEDOM OVER FASCISM
(The Berlin Airlift)

Three years after the end of World War Two, on June 24, 1948, the Soviet Union violated the terms of the armistice which had established zones of occupation for the various sectors of Germany. The United States, Great Britain, France and the Soviet Union each had specific territories of Germany they were to govern while feeding the citizenry and helping to establish a peacetime economy and governance.[293]

---

292 <u>Triumph and Tragedy</u> by Winston Churchill, 1953, pp. 294-295
293 <u>Waging Peace</u> by Dwight D. Eisenhower, 1965, p. 329

Berlin, it had been agreed, would also be partitioned, with the more populous western sector of this huge capital city occupied by British, French and American forces. Berlin itself, was 110 miles inside the portion of eastern Germany which was allotted to Russian occupation and oversight. The western nations were firmly committed to all of Germany being eventually reunited as one nation.

But suddenly, on that June date, the Soviet Union instituted a blockade of all roads, railroads, and canals into the west half of Berlin, leaving 2,225,000 people without the necessities of life which were being brought in by the three Allies. The blockade ended after thirteen months because America stood up to Russian intimidation and tyranny.

President Harry Truman was among those American officials that did not care for the Soviets underhanded dealings in instituting a blockade of west Berlin. Rather than commit to a battle of armaments with the Russians, President Truman ordered an airlift to begin by U.S. Army Air Force cargo planes. Nearly 400 planes flew numerous flights around the clock, back and forth across Germany from an American sector of the country, daily bringing as much as 20 million pounds of food, coal, medicine and other essentials to the residents of west Berlin. The Brits and the Australians also assisted the effort.

What was at stake here? An election was upcoming for mayor, and Russia wanted to see the whole city of Berlin under a Communist mayor, not one city with two different governments. The Soviets used strong arm tactics, letters, and billboard propaganda during the blockade to try to bribe west Berliners into staying home and not voting for conservative candidates in the west Berlin election. Residents of west Berlin received offers by mail of Soviet food ration cards, unlimited electricity, almost a ton of coal, and candy for their children for not voting.[294]

As the December, 1948 west Berlin elections drew near, the Soviet officials pasted their billboard posters over the top of western sector election outdoor advertisements. Three of these Soviet billboards read as follows:

"Whoever Voted for Hitler Voted for War--Whoever Votes Now Votes for War" [295]

"Boycott the Election of the City Splitters" [296]

"Whoever elects the warmongers votes for the return of nights of bombing" [297]

The trouble with the Russian propaganda was that west Berliners did not believe the billboards. The reason for this was that American cargo planes were heard twenty-four hours a day over Berlin. Planes were landing every ninety seconds at either the downtown Templehof Airport, an airport in the British sector of Berlin, or the new airport that U.S. forces had built for the increased supplies

---

294 <u>The Candy Bombers,</u> by Andrei Cherny, 2008, p. 485
295 Ibid., p. 480
296 Ibid., p. 480
297 Ibid., p. 485

being flown in to Berlin. The sound of planes now meant food, not bombs, as in World War Two a few years earlier. As one west Berliner testified:

> *"Early in the morning, when we woke up, the first thing we did was listen to see whether the noise of aircraft engines could be heard. That gave us the certainty that we were not alone, that the whole civilized world took part in the fight for Berlin's freedom."* [298]

Along with food, clothing, fuel and other things, a different kind of airlift had also begun, thanks to the efforts of one kind and diplomatic American Army Air Force pilot named Hal Halvorsen. He, of his own accord, began dropping candy in tiny parachutes to the children which gathered near the final approach to the runway of Berlin's Templehof Airport.

The German children which gathered there had not seen candy in years. Naturally, the news spread around Berlin about the candy being dropped. Back in the United States word of this friendly "candy bomber" spread from coast to coast, which mushroomed the effort.

Within weeks, candy companies like Hershey, Nestle and many others were shipping thousands of pounds of candy gratis for the airlift pilots to drop by parachute to the children of west Berlin. Various clubs such as the Boy Scouts made and shipped crate loads of small cloth parachutes to secure the candy dropped out of the

---

298 <u>The Candy Bombers</u> by Andrei Cherny, 2008, p. 474

cargo planes. More and more of the airlift pilots became involved in this goodwill gesture, and candy from thousands of parachutes was dropped all over the city.

When letters began coming into the American military headquarters at Templehof, and these letters were publicized in America, the hearts of Americans started to melt toward the Berliners, just as the melted chocolate bars in the huge "candy bomber" effort also melted the hearts of Berliners. Here are just three of the letters received from Berliners about the effort:

> *"Dear Uncle Wiggily Wings,,*
> *When yesterday I came from school, I had the happiness to get one of your sweet gifts. First I did not know what do of joy and I could not come home quickly enough, to look at your wonderful things. You cannot think how big the joy was, they all, my brother, and parents stood about me when I opened the strings and fetched out all the chocolate. The delight was very large!*
>
> > *Gratefully,,*
> > *Lieselotte Muller"* [299]

> *"Dear chocolate Uncle,*
> *The oldest of my seven sons had on this day his sixteenth birthday. But when we went out in the morning we were all sad because we had nothing to give him on his special day. But how happily everything turned out! A parachute with chocolate landed on our roof! It was the first sweets for the children*

---

299 The Candy Bombers by Andrei Cherny, 2008, p. 358

in a very long time. Chocolate cannot be bought even with money. My oldest son, a student, came home at eight o'clock and I was able, after all, to give him some birthday happiness. I will gladly return the handkerchief parachute if necessary but I would pray for you to let me keep it as a memento of the Airbridge to Berlin.

With deepest appreciation,
Frau Helga Mueller" [300]

"Mr. Halvorsen, Lt.,
I request you to distribute the attached 12 bags of tiny toy motors to American boys of your native town and hope that they will have much joy on them, just as the Berlin children by your parachute gifts. In the enterprise of my brother-in-law, who manufactures the constructive parts, I obtained some by begging, I am sorry to have got no more as in this moment I am unemployed.
Please regard the mail as a sign of my greatfull acknowledgement of your disinterested action.

Your truly, Hans Drewemann" [301]

The December 5, 1948 west Berlin elections were held, with a huge turnout of 86 percent of Berliners casting their ballots. The most extremely anti-Communist party, the Social Democrats, won more votes than all the other parties combined. The city residents were ecstatic. One Berlin woman wrote:

---

300 Ibid., p. 366
301 The Candy Bombers by Andrei Cherny, 2008, p. 458

"...We feel it's great to be a Berliner. It is wonderful to live in a city that prefers death to slavery, that has decided to suffer more deprivations rather than dictatorship." [302]

Because the Berlin airlift continued to supply the needs of the west half of Berlin in their entirety, and because of the Communist's loss of the Berlin mayoral election to democratic candidates, the Berlin blockade was given up by the Soviet Union on April 12, 1949. Trucks, trains, barges, buses and cars once again moved freely in and out of west Berlin.

This is a good example of how people will choose freedom rather than Fascist tyranny if given the choice. The citizens of west Berlin, who had been under the Nazi yoke for twelve years, came to realize that yielding to Russian Fascism would keep them under the same horrid yoke as Nazi Fascism. And happily, the entire fragmented country of Germany was finally unyoked from the Soviet Union and reunited as a free, sovereign nation in 1990.

Unfortunately today, America no longer possesses the strong and brave leadership that it enjoyed under President Harry Truman, who was not afraid to stand up to the Soviet Union when they blockaded Berlin. While some of his military leaders back then were prepared to go to war with the Soviet Union, many of the politicians were ready to back down and allow the Soviets to blackmail their way into controlling the entire capital city of vanquished Germany. But Harry Truman played the man and employed the huge fleet of cargo planes, which flew a total of 92 million miles bringing food and aid

---

302 Ibid., p. 490

to Berlin. This resulted in the Soviet Fascists backing down in their cowardly efforts to harass and intimidate their intended prey.

People Fleeing Fascism
(The Berlin Wall)

The Soviet Union was the occupying power of east Germany and the eastern half of Berlin at the close of World War Two. These territories were experiencing a continuous mass exodus from Russian rule. From 1945 until 1961, 3.5 million East Germans fled Russian Communist oppression. Those who left the country were the best educated people, including doctors, engineers and others that knew a better life awaited them in a free society.

Consequently, the Soviets proceeded in 1961 to construct a wall separating east Germany (Soviet territory) from west Germany (western Allies territory) to stop people from leaving. The wall also split the entire capital city of Berlin between the west half of the city, governed by the United States, France and England. and the east half controlled by the Soviets. The wall halted nearly all emigration out of East Germany and east Berlin. Please note the direction of migration. People were not trying to flee <u>into</u> communist-held east Berlin and eastern Germany, but, they were trying to get <u>out</u>!

The official name of the Berlin Wall, given by the Soviets, was the "Anti-Fascist Protection Rampart."[303] The name itself was laughable, as the human traffic trying to flee Fascism was from the Soviet side to the free, western Allies side. About 200 people

---

303 https://en.wikipedia.org/wiki/Berlin_Wall

attempting to flee to freedom in and around Berlin were shot and killed by armed Soviet guards at the Berlin Wall during the approximate twenty year life of the Berlin Wall.

A journalist named Eric Sevareid wrote about the fact that millions of people around the world wish to come to America because of freedom. His statement about what freedom really is captures what it means to be free:

> *"It is so strange--these ordinary, unlettered people know in their bones what freedom is, even if their intellectuals do not. Freedom is the condition of feeling like one's self."* [304]

The Berlin Wall stood until 1990, when changes in the political climate of Europe called for the reunification of Germany. The wall was torn down. However, the Berlin Wall is emblematic of the fact that life under Fascism or Communism--essentially the same thing--is something that people would like to leave if they could manage to do so.

TODAY'S NEWS: IS IT PROPAGANDA OR TRUTH?

This question needs to be asked in our day for at least two reasons. First, because we have a national government in Washington that has become altogether too powerful. Secondly, the motives and goals of our leaders have become suspect as to the future good of the United States. There is an arrogance apparent in the speeches and pronouncements of President Barack Obama, various career politicians in Congress, and liberal justices of the U.S. Supreme Court.

---

304 <u>Not So Wild a Dream</u> by Eric Sevareid, 1946, p. xvii

The various national news outlets compound the search for truth in that they do little or nothing to question our elected leaders, or to present opposing views of what our politicians say and do. One could easily conclude that the media outlets themselves are controlled by or expressly part of the Federal government. They are certainly in concert with the parties in power.

America appears to be headed toward mind control by a news media that is aimed at making fools of its audience. Substance or truth in our news is questionable. This is not an exaggerated view. Consider how mind control came about in another western nation in history. A noted American journalist who lived in Germany through the first eight years of Hitler's reign, wrote of methods of Nazi mind control. Truth disseminated in the news was expressed in terms of a typical German man this writer called Willie:

> *"Hitler and Goebbels have slapped Willi into a rigid mental quarantine. They control what he is taught, what he reads, what he sees and what he is told. By this system, officially known as 'Public Enlightenment and Propaganda,' they have in time reached the point where they can even control what Willi thinks.[305]*

America is the same way today. Who masterminds and controls the reports of happenings in our world today which are presented as news? In this 21st century, journalism has mutated into a quest for riches and/or fame tied to various liberal causes which are attention-getting, such as discrimination. One needs to look for the hidden agenda behind every story that is brought out as news.

305 <u>This Is The Enemy</u> by Frederick Oechsner, 1942, p. 242

Conservative-leaning news media outlets are demonized, marginalized and ridiculed.

Television news broadcasting is strictly centered around creating and maintaining viewership by creating public opinion, not just shaping it! Therefore, the new stories are sensational. The latest bad news is forever termed "breaking news." Ironically, the so-called breaking news is repeated for days and weeks so that the viewers opinions become more and more aligned with the tenor of the one-sided rendition of the ad nausea television news story presented.

Adolf Hitler controlled all news media in Germany and occupied territories. Newspapers were very important news outlets in those days. He theorized that there were three kinds of readers. First, there were those readers that believed nothing they read. Second, there were readers that believed little of what they read. Thirdly was the largest group--the kind of people that were the least intelligent, and therefore believed everything they read. Hitler stated that he concentrated on only the last group of people! Consequently news served to disseminate his propaganda was aimed specifically at this gullible group. This so-called news was given out with certain "catch words" or phrases, **repeated endlessly**, to gain the desired support of the masses.[306]

Whatever the issue, news today is disseminated by television and other media which is contrived by a rule of thumb. That rule being, the story must guarantee controversy or a diversity of opinions which divide people for or against issues. As with Hitler,

---

306 <u>This Is The Enemy</u> by Frederick Oechsner, 1942, pp. 243-244

"catch words" or phrases used today, such as "black lives matter" or "climate change," are continually repeated by the news media in order to bring about a desired way of thinking.

The reiteration of the phrase "black lives matter" seems to imply that many people do not think this to be true, thus, conflict and division have been created. "Climate change," another commonly used phrase in the news, is nearly accepted as fact rather than theory by many people today simply because they have heard it repeated so often. Some government officials, such as Secretary of State John Kerry, actually refer to those who oppose the theory of "climate change" as "climate change deniers." That phrase implies that "climate change" is in fact the truth and to think otherwise is wrong. It sounds rather like Propaganda Minister Joseph Goebbels does it not? The creation of camps pro and con by television news media and government is promulgated on purpose, by design. The design is to hold the attention of Americans on unimportant or inconsequential matters, while important issues such as illegal immigration, failed Federal programs, Islamic terrorism, abortion, and fiscal irresponsibility (we are as a nation essentially bankrupt) are not dealt with as needed for the well being of America. This is how propaganda and the demoralization of a country works.

Hitler's propaganda ministry termed this tactic "the red herring"[307] because it allowed insignificant issues to mask serious happenings which were being kept under wraps. There will be consequences for America because Americans are basically in the dark as to the critical issues of our day. What you don't know can hurt you!

---

307 <u>This Is The Enemy</u> by Frederick Oechsner, 1942, p. 252

There are consequences also for lying to people. Take for example the Rachel Carson book entitled "The Silent Spring," published in 1962. What a furor the book caused. This book claimed that the anti-malarial chemical pesticide called DDT was causing bird's eggshells to be so soft that they would break when the parent bird sat on them, and the world would soon have no birds! This book led to a worldwide ban on DDT within a decade.

Unfortunately, the ban on DDT led to the reappearance of many deaths by mosquito-born malaria, which had been nearly wiped out by the use of DDT. DDT had also been used extensively in World War Two to kill lice, which spread deadly typhus to humans. Lice afflicted millions of prisoners of war, refugees, and inmates of concentration camps.

Since the global banning of DDT thirty years ago, about three million people worldwide have died every year from malaria. These deaths were totally preventable! The claim that DDT was harmful to birds and their eggs has been shown scientifically to be completely false. Bad ideas like a ban on DDT don't go away, even when proven false![308]

It bears to be repeated. Lying propaganda presented as news, and repeated often enough, can cause great harm. Within the last decade or so, the government through the news media, convinced people that using our food crops to make ethanol as an automotive fuel would "reduce our dependence on foreign oil." That was

---

308 <u>The Black Book of the American Left</u> by D. Horowitz, 2013, p. 383

a great deception. Since then, our government has not only stood in the way of our own oil development and production, but as a consequence of using our food crops for ethanol, prices of food and other related products have soared. Worse yet, ethanol reduces miles per gallon in cars, and damages small engines. Will this bad idea go away?

News stories repeated over and over cause many listeners to accept what is reported as truth, whether or not truth is involved. What is needed today is real truth in reporting, rather than the promulgation of specific groups' agendas which are put forth repeatedly by the ever-controlling news media.

The "global warming" theme in news stories has been far spreading. A large zoo displaying a colorful sign by the polar bear's exhibit requested contributions to save the polar bear's natural habitat in the Arctic, which was widely reported to be shrinking due to global warming. In the final analysis, the opposite was actually true but since the truth did not support the global warming argument, the news media simply dropped the issue. Unless politically correct, error is not admitted or brought to light in news reporting.

The free world today, especially the United States, is in dire need of honest news reporting in print and broadcasting. As Job said, "how forcible are right words." The Fascist enemy worldwide is Islam. The atrocities committed by Muslims are termed "terrorist attacks" rather than "Islamic terrorist attacks" because of political correctness. This is dishonesty. Truth is nearly fallen in the streets.

THE OPPRESSED HATE FASCISM!

Call it ill will. Call it the urge to be free. Whatever you want to call it, free people who are oppressed and cast into servitude against their will are going to eventually gain their freedom. Consider the following statement about Nazi Fascism and the similarity it has to Islam's goal of world domination:

> *"You don't have to be profound to conclude that the rule of brute force now exercised by the Germans over the occupied territories can never last very long. For despite complete military and police power, which the Germans admittedly have, you cannot for ever rule over foreign European peoples who hate and detest you. The success of Hitler's "new order" in Europe is therefore doomed even before it is set up. The Nazis, of course, who have never troubled to study European history but are guided by a primitive Germanic tribal urge of conquest with no thought for the possible consequences, think that they are well on their way to installing a European "new order" which will be dominated by Germany for the greater good of Germany for all time."* [309]

The human spirit can only be crushed for so long. Here is the atmosphere of the French people just a few months after the Nazis took over their country in 1940:

> *"One German equals fifty Frenchmen. For every German who died by violence, fifty Frenchmen must lose their lives... Innocent hostages are still being arrested and murdered on the*

---

309 <u>Berlin Diary</u> by William Shirer, 1941, p. 531

slightest pretext. But for every victim, ten, a hundred will rise up. For there is something that cannot be killed, not by all the guns in the world; that cannot be blown up, not by all the bombs in the world; that cannot be crushed, not by all the tanks in existence. Call it soul." [310]

The people of Poland suffered untold hardship under Nazi Fascism in World War Two. Every fifth or sixth person in a jail or certain village would be shot for each Nazi Gestapo agent killed in Poland.[311] Mass deportations sent millions of people to work or death camps. The entire agricultural production of Poland was taken away to Germany, with the deliberate design for mass starvation of the Polish people.[312] For example, Germans in Poland were allotted 750 grams (1 pound, 10 ounces) of meat per week per person, while native Poles were issued food coupons that allowed them to buy just 60 grams (2.1 ounces) of meat per person per week.[313]

Thousands of babies born to Polish couples whose marriage was secret, that is, not approved in advance as racially pure by the Gestapo, were stolen away from the parents never to be seen again![314]

"The people who did not live under German domination will never be able to gauge the strength of this hatred and will find it difficult to understand that every moral law, convention or

310 <u>Underground Europe</u> by Curt Riess, 1942, pp.91-92
311 <u>Story Of A Secret State</u> by Jan Karski, 1944, p. 255
312 Ibid., p. 249
313 <u>Underground Europe</u> by Curt Riess, 1942, p. 199
314 <u>Story Of A Secret State</u> by Jan Karski, 1944, p. 256

restriction on impulses simply disappeared. Nothing remained but the desperation of an animal caught in a trap. We fought back against an enemy determined to destroy us. Poland snarled and clawed back at its oppressors like a wounded cat. I doubt if such a state has existed in large collectivities since the time of Christ."[315]

Freedom loving people must fight if they are to remain free. History itself bears this out, when viewed in light of the greed and lust that Fascists have had, and still have today, for control.

---

315 Ibid., p. 258

CHAPTER 16

Concluding thoughts

─────

HERE BELOW IS A DIRECT quote from a well known journalist about the character of Nazi Germany. Is it not an apt description of the nature and behavior of the character of Islam today which is plainly evident--but not admitted--in our world?:

I certainly would not have gone into Germany when I did to find out more about the Nazis. Anyone who had seen them there since 1923 should know all he needed to know about this collection of hoodlums. And, in any case, who does not realize that they are America's mortal enemies? Therefore, it seems a little absurd at this late date to find so much written about the threat of the Nazis to free men. If there was ever an evident and banal subject this is it.

German refugees, especially the more sophisticated and brittle ones, offend America's intelligence and belabor the obvious when they tell us to beware the Nazis. We need no warning against Nazis. The Nazis are liars, thieves, murderers, and egomaniacs. No man in his right senses, American or European, would trust them as far as he could throw an anvil. We are at war with them, and we will never stop fighting the Nazis until the whole Nazi hierarchy is pounded to pieces, from Hitler down. There is not the slightest chance of England's or America's making peace with the Nazis. In the words of Winston Churchill, our idea is to 'beat them to the ground.' "[316]

Those that make leagues with Fascists, thinking to benefit, also suffer. Remember what happened to Italy when considering what to think about Fascism, whether it be German, Japanese, Italian, Russian, or Muslim:

"After 20 years under the boot of Mussolini and his cohorts, Italians with any regard for facts thought they knew all there was to know about Fascism--its murder or exile of all political opponents, its anti-Semitism, its suppression of all media of independent expression, its systematic looting of business and its regimentation of labor, its perversion of the arts, its terror-ism of Italian nationals who had changed their citizenship, its interference in the domestic affairs of foreign countries, its insistence upon the right of the state to regulate every detail of the private lives of the people, its insistence upon 'the noth-ingness of the individual.' After Mussolini turned the country over to Germany, in the hope of sharing Hitler's glory and loot, it learned that the Italian fascists were novices. The Germans so regarded them, they never looked upon Italians as partners, but as slaves."[317]

---

316 <u>Men in Motion</u> by Henry J. Taylor 1943, p. 69

317 <u>This Must Not Happen Again! The Black Book of Fascist Horror</u> by Clark Kinnaird, 1945, p. 90

Fascism in any form enslaves the subjects which must live under it. There is no room for the thoughts of the individual. The State is always uppermost and the supposed common good is supreme.

It was thought by many that Nazi Germany could not be beaten militarily. It was also said by military experts that a country could not fight a war on two fronts. Germany initiated war on two different fronts in World War Two, but lost the war. America, leading the Allied forces, though forced to fight the war on two fronts, still won! How was this possible?

Was the war won through appeasement? No, not in any way. It cost America dearly in human lives as well as materially. But Fascism had to be fought using force because Hitler's Nazi Fascists desired to rule the world by force. U.S. Army General Dwight Eisenhower, Supreme Commander, Allied Expeditionary Forces, sent out this directive to all fighting forces in the battle against Nazi fascism in 1944:

"You will enter the continent of Europe and, in conjunction with the other Allied Nations, undertake operations aimed at the heart of Germany and the destruction of her Armed Forces. This purpose of destroying enemy forces was always our guiding principle."[318]

The enemies of Fascism know that Fascist enterprises must be stopped. And the leaders of the murderous Fascist system must be punished. Because of the atrocities committed by Nazis in World

---

318 <u>Crusade in Europe</u> by Dwight D. Eisenhower 1948, p. 225

War Two, the three great powers of Great Britain, the United States and the Soviet Union developed a declaration of intent, warning the German nation that perpetrators of war crimes and crimes against humanity would be tried and punished. This was done in October of 1943, nearly two years before the war ended. It was hoped that Germany and its Axis power Japan would have second thoughts before committing more atrocities such as had already been widely documented in the occupied nations of the world.

In part, the three Allied powers declaration stated:

"At the time of the granting of any armistice to any government which may be set up in Germany, those German officers and men and members of the Nazi Party who have been responsible for or have taken a consenting part in the atrocities, massacres and executions will be sent back to the countries in which their abominable deeds were done, in order that they may be judged and punished according to the laws of these liberated countries and the free Governments which will be erected therein..."[319]

KILLING COPS AND COPTICS

Islamic jihad has been carried out in Egypt by various terrorist groups for decades. Egypt is the birthplace of the Muslim Brotherhood, a group which Egypt Premier Abdul Nasser tried to stamp out unsuccessfully. From the 1980's right up until the present day Islamic terrorist factions of one stripe or another have

---

319 <u>Closing the Ring</u> by Winston Churchill, 1951, p. 297

murdered police, state officials, and Coptic Christians in Egypt. These violent acts were carried out in hopes of stirring up enough civil unrest for the people to clamor for the creation of a strong, centralized Islamic government to rule Egypt.

Since Coptic Christians are automatically on the list of enemies of Islam, there was no need to pronounce them as "kafir" or guilty of "impiety", which in Islam brands people and governments considered apostate to the faith of Islam. But, in Egypt, violence against Coptics increased whenever there was a convenient excuse to kill. On one occasion, Coptic Christians in Egypt were murdered because of an outrageous rumor that they had sprayed Muslim women's veils with a secret formula that caused the veil to show a Christian cross on it when the veil was washed.[320]

However, for the past several decades, in Egypt, as in Algeria, Bosnia and France, the seemingly endless murders of academics, doctors, intellectuals, journalists and even foreign tourists have worked against Islamic terrorism, not for it. Moderate, non-violent Muslims have refused to support violent Muslim extremists or take up their cause.

But there are plenty of other countries where the cause of Islamic jihad is embraced successfully due to population explosion, racial hatred, hate speech, and the philosophy of martyrdom for Allah. Remember, both major factions of Islam, Sunnis and Shias grow and export the fever to kill "infidels." The cause for jihad

320 Jihad: The Trail of Political Islam by Gilles Kepel, 2002, p. 283

often mutates depending on the latest "fatwa" (writing) that some "imam" (Muslim cleric) has written for or against some aspect of the Koran. These fatwas precipitate violence both within and without the Muslim realm.

Until Islam is recognized as a Fascist political ideology and dealt with accordingly, country by country from which the violence springs, the terror, hijackings, kidnappings, beheadings, outright murder, suicide bombings, rocket attacks, and threats against non-Muslims will not cease. Unprovoked rocket bomb attacks into Israel now number in the tens of thousands coming from neighboring Muslims in Syria and Muslim-occupied Palestinian Gaza, which seek the eradication of the Jewish State.

In America today, multiculturalism, pantheism, political correctness and non-discrimination are absolutes. There are no elected officials in Washington who are squarely facing and dealing with the unending problem of Islamic Fascism which seeks to destroy America. Instead, we try to appease, compromise or buy America's way out of trouble.

NAZIS AND MUSLIMS IN THE U.S. ARMY

America and Great Britain had enough good sense to forbid men whose allegiance was to Nazi Germany, to join up with their military forces fighting Germany. It would have been suicidal. But that is how undiscerning and utterly stupid America's national leadership is today, allowing Muslims, both American born and foreign born, in our U.S. armed forces. Islam is the enemy of America.

A case in point. Ali Mohammed, an Egyptian born Muslim, came to the United States under a program for military personnel of other countries to train in America. In 1986, our convoluted laws and leadership allowed him to join the U.S. Army! He graduated from Special Forces Officers School and obtained a security clearance for secret Army documents. Later, it was discovered in the raid of another suspected Muslim terrorist, that Ali Mohammed had photocopied and passed on to al Qaeda-connected terrorists, secret Army documents showing the locations and plans for U.S. Special Forces operations in the Middle East.

In 1989, Mohammed left the U.S. Army and began training Islamic militants in guerrilla warfare right here on our shores, in New Jersey. Two years later, living in California, he made frequent trips to Sudan and Afghanistan, as a top aide to Osama bin Laden. He went about setting up terrorist training camps in foreign lands and began training terrorists. Finally, in 1998, the FBI had enough evidence against him to arrest and convict him of terrorist activities.[321] Our government is simply not up to the mark on anti-terrorism, by the design of our dishonest leaders.

The point here is, America has not come to grips with the fact that individuals who identify themselves as Muslim must be excluded from our armed services. This is absolutely necessary because the <u>stated goal of Islam is</u>, the destruction of the United States, pure and simple. "Declared enemies of the

---

321 <u>American Jihad: The Terrorists Living Among Us</u> by Steven Emerson, 2002, pp. 55-60

United States must be taken at their word."[322] Let us not forget about the Muslim U.S. Army officer in Fort Hood, Texas who gunned down 14 people in cold blood as a further reminder of this fact.

More Muslim violence and bloodshed are planned both here and abroad. As Americans we enjoy many freedoms granted by our Constitution. Islamic terrorists in our country likewise benefit from these freedoms, but they use them rather for evil and the shedding of blood. A group of Muslims arrested in the United States for assisting the Hezbollah terrorist organization, had plans to acquire the following when arrested: stun guns, mine-detection equipment, advanced aircraft analysis and design software, night vision goggles, and blasting equipment.[323] All these items are dangerous in the hands of terrorists. Do such items as these sound like elements of a lawful, peaceful religion that someone wants to tell you about?

Elected officials of the Federal government of the United States continually try to appease the Muslim world where any conflict exists, ignoring the clinical fact that paranoid behavior such as Fascist Muslims exhibit, cannot be appeased. For example, American armed forces fighting in Islamic countries such as Afghanistan are not permitted to receive Christian Bibles while in residence there. American news media have reported the burning of Bibles by the U.S. Army in Afghanistan lest they should fall into the hands of Afghan citizens and offend them. By the same token, a sentence

---

322 Endgame: The Blueprint for Victory in the War on Terror by Lt. Gen. T. McInerny & Maj. Gen. Paul Vallely, 2004, p. 91

323 American Jihad: The Terrorists Living Among Us by Steven Emerson, 2002, p. 36

of death by Muslims awaits anyone who would dare to burn the Muslim's Koran in today's world. Fascism always asserts its absolute rights!

The time has also come for America to also receive payment, either in oil or in cash, for sending aid to nations troubled with Islamic violence. Whether our aid is sending military troops, armed drones or the training of other nation's troops, America is in deep financial trouble and can no longer afford to play the part of the rich uncle. We delivered Iraq from Saddam Hussein, and should have been compensated, likewise with oil-rich Kuwait.

The domestic threat to the United States from Islamic Fascism is increasing as Muslims speak peace but talk with their swords and assault rifles. During the George W. Bush administration, U.S. Senator Feinstein and other Democrats in Congress complained that conservative watchdogs were scrutinizing Islamic officials who were scheduled to meet with the President. The criticism of President Bush meeting with militant Islamic organizations went unheeded, despite known terrorist connections. Warnings were ignored:

> *"...even though leaders of prominent "mainstream" Islamic organizations such as the Council on American Islamic Relations (CAIR) have been convicted of terrorist activities, while others have been linked by the Federal Bureau of Investigation to a formally-organized network of the Muslim Brotherhood, the fountainhead of Islamic terrorism."* [324]

---

324 <u>The Black Book of the American Left</u> by D. Horowitz, 2013, p. 322

There are multiplied enemies of freedom and capitalism within our shores. Some are Muslims. Others are antagonists, such as film-makers who pass themselves off as peace or human rights activists, while disseminating blatantly Marxist and anti-American propaganda movies. Is anyone dumb enough to think that our own leaders planned the Muslim terror attack of September 11, 2001? But such ideas are put forth.

Thus, America is undermined internally, and hindered from developing strategies to deal with Islam because America's own motives are brought into question. We as a nation are more and more susceptible to the lies of Fascist Islam: by sedition, by divisiveness, and even by propaganda against the good which America tries to do for other countries.

Islam is hard at work trying to change the landscape of America into that of an Islamic State. Very ornate Muslim mosques have been built and are being built across America, financed largely by Saudi Arabia.[325] Very subtly, Islam preys on the overwhelming political correctness and tolerance of our day, which forbids criticism of minority groups of any kind. Never mind the terrorist violence committed in the name of Islam.

Islam uses psychological weapons in our American culture, not just on battle fields. The express purpose is to wear down the enemy. Here is a description given in a book written about such Fascist psychological warfare methods 70 years ago:

---

325 Ibid., p. 397

> *"Applied psychology as a weapon of war means propaganda intended to influence the attitude of nations at war. It is essential to attack the enemy nation in its weak spots--and what nation has not its weak spots--to undermine and break down its resistance, and to convince it that it is being deceived, misled and brought to destruction by its own government."* [326]

Yes, America is asleep about Islamic Fascism

Is it possible to ignore immense human suffering caused by violent aggression? One can almost become numb to it, because our daily news has frequent reports of murders and mass murders by Islamists.

Muslim tactics vary as needed when dealing with different nations of people. In many countries, their own firearms and long knives do all the talking. Entire unarmed civilizations are brought under the Islamic yoke through violence and the threat of further violence.

The threat of kidnapping, sexual slavery or death by ISIS is causing untold masses of Muslims to flee from countries such as Iraq and Syria right now. Yet, a skeptic would have to ask if such migration into non-Muslim parts of Europe isn't really part of a larger plan to spread Islam? When you consider that many Muslim nations surrounding Iraq have sufficient military means to escalate the war against ISIS, why don't they join in the battle against them? Or why do they not offer Muslims safe haven?

In America, in large measure, Islamic leaders labor to teach that Islam is a religion of peace, all the while jihad is being conducted

---

326 <u>Paper Bullets</u> by Leo Margolin 1946, p. 31

but not talked about. Fascism is always spread by tactics that best fit in each people group to be mastered. But world news tells the story.

American involvement has not stopped terrorism abroad. The first Gulf War in 1990-1991 cost the United States about 350 soldier's lives and $60 billion. Oil rich Kuwait, was delivered at our expense, with borrowed money American taxpayers must repay with interest.

In 2003, United States armed forces delivered Iraq from dictatorial rule. There were 4,491 American soldiers killed in the Iraq war, which cost the United States $1.7 trillion according to a study by Brown University. Were we paid for our effort, in oil or in cash? No. Terrorists know America is vain enough to become bankrupt fighting Islamic Fascism.

CBS News reported in May, 2004, that the U.S. government under President Bush sent $12 billion (not million) in crisp $100 bills to Iraq for the new government called the "Coalition Provisional Authority." The money was flown into Baghdad in 21 flights by U.S. Air Force C-130 cargo planes. All of that money subsequently disappeared! It is hard to imagine that our Federal government simply lost track of $12 billion, and has never determined where the money went. This is an example of government malfeasance by which America is plagued and foredoomed.

By way of comparison as to how much money $12 billion represents, the new World Trade Center, built to replace the twin towers destroyed by Islamic terrorists, cost $3.9 billion to rebuild. The new buildings were paid for in large measure by New York taxpayers, higher bridge and ferry tolls, and high rents.

America's very costly involvement in Iraq over an eight year period has not solved Iraq's problems. President Obama made a far fetched statement about our withdrawal from Iraq, in a speech on December 14, 2011:

> *"...But we're leaving behind a sovereign, stable and self-reliant Iraq, with a representative government that was elected by its people."* [327]

That statement is false. Iraq today is as unstable, and rife with open warfare, as it was before America intervened and "helped" establish a new government in that country in 2003. As of the summer of 2015, the Islamic State terror group known as ISIS is in power in a sizeable chunk of Iraq, and their fighters are within 70 miles of the capital city of Baghdad.[328] This certainly is not an indication that Iraq was left sovereign and stable, as stated by President Obama.

America's involvement fighting Islamic terrorism on foreign soil will continue to be fruitless unless a large, unified, ongoing multi-national effort is waged to solve the problem. Many Muslim groups and nations naturally resent the interference of American military in conducting war against Muslims of any sort on their soil. In their view, it is an American invasion. Yet, Muslims have no

---

327 The Complete Infidel's Guide to ISIS by Robert Spencer, 2015, p.115
328 The Complete Infidel's Guide to ISIS by Robert Spencer, 2015, p.288

problem attacking western nations, apparently believing it is their duty to do so.

Take into account some of the large Islamic oil empires: Qatar, Kuwait, the United Arab Emirates and Saudi Arabia. All have larger per person gross domestic product (a measure of wealth and purchasing power) than the United States. They have the wealth to muster a military force capable of eliminating all Muslim terrorist groups. But rich Muslim nations do not care, in fact, quite the opposite is true. Saudi Arabia with its massive oil wealth casts itself to the world as rich, powerful and peace loving. But Saudi Arabia is a huge part of the problem:

> *"The vast majority of American mosques are funded with Saudi Arabian money, and most of the funders subscribe to the Saudi doctrine of Wahhabism, an eighteenth-century ideology of extreme purity that supports the spread of Islam through violence."* [329]

Everyone knows what the terrorist group ISIS will use their wealth for, of which they are currently acquiring through violence and theft in Iraq, Syria and elsewhere. The inaction of Muslim nations in stopping Muslim terrorism speaks louder than words. The truth is, Islam is no religion at all! It is a Fascist geopolitical ideology under the guise of religion, that embraces expansion of its control toward worldwide domination by violence, threats and demands. As with Hitler's Fascism, each demand if granted only leads to more and higher demands. And there are many Islamic jihad players.

---

329 <u>American Jihad: The Terrorists Living Among Us</u> by Steven Emerson, 2002, pp. 41

Psychological Warfare:
Non-Violent Islamic Methods

1. Islamic demonstrations and a war of nerves

Islam of course uses Nazi methods of violence and murder to intimidate and cower opposition. But Islam also uses non-violent demonstrations to spread the notion that Muslims are victims of discrimination and intolerance.

When Fascists hate others, they allege the opposite to be true, that others hate them. In mid-July, 2015, about 200 Muslims rallied in Sydney, and other Australian cities under the banner of "Reclaim Australia," which claims to be a non-racist group advocating tolerance and equality among all races and religions. However, a much larger crowd of non-Muslims, knowing the truth of the matter, held counter-demonstrations, condemning the Muslim demonstrations as "racism, Fascism, and Islamophobia."[330]

Victimhood, growing in popularity, is a pretense for non-acceptance of the strange and savage attributes of Islamic peoples. This is especially true in countries where Muslims are very much in the minority. Should the violence that is committed in the name of Allah by Muslims everywhere on the planet be ignored? Muslims are simultaneously demonstrating and marching peaceably in some places, hope that people will overlook and disregard the murderous, intimidating, Fascist behavior of militant Islam, and the blood spilled by Islamic terror. It is a strange combination for Muslims to

---

330 http://islamist-watch.org/blog/2015/07/reclaim-australia-demonstrations-and-counter

expect acceptance like any other minority while at the same time they rage on with their violence.

The murders of innocent people right here in the United States is never really addressed by the approximately three million so-called non-violent Muslims in America. There are two possible reasons for this. One is that apologizing or expressing sorrow and remorse seemingly negates the non-violent portrayal in which they are attempting to cast and theatricize themselves.

The other reason is, Muslims of any stripe are not really opposed to the bloodshed of "infidels." If Muslims were expressing remorse or opposition to murder, those Muslims would be ostracized for impiety by militant Muslims in the Mideast, where the origins, the birthplace, the cradle, the true face of Islam is exhibited by violence, bloodshed and aggression.

This is precisely how Adolf Hitler came to power in Nazi Germany. There was quiet and peace offered to German society if Germans caved in and began accepting the National Socialist Party (Nazis) as a legitimate political force. The <u>known threat</u> of violence by Hitler's hired brown shirts when Nazi's marched, saw more and more people afraid to not give the stiff-armed salutes of "Heil Hitler" to the political party called the Nazis. But once in office, exercising unlimited powers, Germany and the whole world suffered immensely from Adolf Hitler and his thugs for the next twelve years.

On September 27, 2007, John Howard, the Prime Minister of Australia gave a speech aimed at Muslims, in which he made it no secret that Australia was a Christian nation, and that the country was not going to be changed through the mechanism of multiculturalism that is being advanced by liberals and foreigners:

> *"This culture has been developed over two centuries of struggles, trials and victories by millions of men and women who have sought freedom."*
>
> *"We speak mainly ENGLISH, not Spanish, Lebanese, Arabic, Chinese, Japanese, Russian, or any other language. Therefore, if you wish to become part of our society, learn the language!"*
>
> *"Most Australians believe in God. This is not some Christian, right wing, political push, but a fact, because Christian men and women, on Christian principles, founded this nation, and this is clearly documented. It is certainly appropriate to display it on the walls of our schools. If God offends you, then I suggest you consider another part of the world as your new home, because God is part of our culture."*
>
> *"We will accept your beliefs, and will not question why. All we ask is that you accept ours, and live in harmony and peaceful enjoyment with us."*
>
> *"This is OUR COUNTRY, OUR LAND, and OUR LIFESTYLE, and we will allow you every opportunity to enjoy all this. But once you are done complaining, whining, and griping about Our Flag, Our Pledge, Our Christian beliefs, or Our Way of Life, I highly encourage you take advantage of one other great Australian freedom, 'THE RIGHT TO LEAVE'."*
>
> *"If you aren't happy here then LEAVE. We didn't force you to come here. You asked to be here. So accept the country YOU accepted."*[331]

---

331 http://elhambinai.blogspot.com/2007/09/prime-minister-of-australia-john-howard.html

This bold statement by the Australian Prime Minister needs to be made in these United States. To pander to Islam or to fear it, is to succumb to their underhanded, violent and sadistic methods.

Hitler invented tactics Muslims use today. Hitler called it nerve war! He also termed it the "walls of Jericho" technique.[332] It was described as circling your opponents walls with trumpets tooting only moderately in volume. Afterwards, you look around to see if the walls are trembling yet. If not, you go around again, trumpeting about threats of war, violations against a minority race, insults to ones race, and other accusations intimating the outbreak of war. Seldom, it was said, was there the need to go around the walls seven times, as the walls came down with these nerve war tactics. Such threats had to be backed up by the ability to conduct actual physical violence and terror. And they were backed up by real terror! We all know and have seen and heard many accounts of Islamic terror. The threat of Islamic violence is blatantly real.

2. ISLAMIC SUBVERSION ON COLLEGE CAMPUSES

In America today, Islam is working in non-violent means for acceptance as a "religion of peace," ignoring the Islamic violence occurring around the planet. What group among Americans, would be most likely to believe that Islam is peaceful, when 1.6 billion Muslims in the world subscribe to a so-called holy war against all non-Muslims? **American college students, that's who!** In any generation since about the end of World War One, college students in western nations rise up for new or radical causes.

---

332 <u>This is the Enemy</u> by Frederick Oechsner, 1942, pp. 9-10

The naivete of college students is due to inexperience as to the realities of aggressor nations against free people. Because of the great bloodshed of World War One, opposition to any and all war was a consequence in England and elsewhere. For example, the Oxford University of England's student debating society passed a resolution overwhelmingly in 1933, that "this house will in no circumstances fight for its King and Country."[333] Keep in mind, this was 15 years after the end of World War One.

However, beginning in the summer of 1940, German war planes began the unprovoked bombing and killing of unarmed civilians of the city of London. This act of bloodthirsty aggression quickly cured British college students of the mindset to refuse to serve their country in war. Colleges were verily emptied of their male students to go fight against Nazi Germany in World War Two from that time on.

In the 1960's, American colleges were the hotbed of opposition to involvement in the Vietnam war. This took the form of protests, sit-ins, bombings, even the takeover of college and university buildings to protest that war. There were other issues, including the sexual revolution, legalizing drugs and more which interplayed with a changing nation in the throes of abandoning traditional Christian values.

Students in today's liberal arts colleges are also indoctrinated by the very liberal slant of college professors. There is a near-total absence of conservative views at colleges and universities in our day. This is because of a tendency in colleges and universities for

---

333 <u>Is Germany Incurable</u> by Richard Brickner, M.D., 1943, p. 203

tenured professors to be both independent of public opinion and very liberal in their points of view. College students are generally young people who are inexperienced in life, and are prone to adopting extreme views and causes where both sides of an issue are not examined.

Today, Islamic extremists are pouring money into their cause by propagandizing American college students on college campuses. Islam is presented as a victimized, misunderstood, minority religion which is being persecuted unjustly. The message they give is the lie that their mystic god Allah, is simply another name for the LORD, which is the name of the Christian's God. They also pass on the bold lie that the Koran is another holy book of god. The trouble with all of that is that it is simply not true. But most college students do not know and understand the Christian Bible, though they might identify themselves with the Christian faith.

Please note, that one of the mantras of Islam states **God has no son**. Thus, Jesus Christ is hailed in Islam as a prophet, nothing more. But, the Christian Bible teaches emphatically that the LORD, God of heaven and earth, has declared that His Son Jesus Christ, would and did take upon Himself the form of a man, and was born of a virgin woman. Jesus lived expressly that he might voluntarily die a substitutionary death on a cruel Roman cross to offer reconciliation with God to all who would confess their sinful condition and accept Jesus Christ as Savior.

The Bible claims that faith in Jesus Christ is the only way to an eternity in Heaven with God, and that those who deny the Son of God, Jesus Christ, are anathema, meaning cursed of God because they reject God's remedy for the sins of sinful human beings. The Bible also makes it quite clear that it is a complete book, the full revelation of God to man, and there is none other. The Bible states clearly that there are deplorable plagues forthcoming to anyone who adds to or takes away from the Holy Bible.

While Islam declares death to the enemies of Allah, quite a different message is professed in the Christian faith. The Bible commands men to love their enemies and pray for them. Which doctrine would sound more reasonable to a neutral observer?

Some would claim that the Christian beliefs are narrow minded. The way to Heaven is in fact described in the Christian Bible as a narrow gate of which few therein enter. People have a free will to accept or reject the God of the Bible. Christians, unlike Muslims, do not brandish guns and swords to force their beliefs, under threat of death, upon others.

Diversity is the cry of liberals and lunatic followers of perverse sexual habits. It is a banner under which nearly any human behavior is paraded and toleration demanded; whereas in days gone by these actions would have been restricted, refused and even outlawed in this once moral United States of America. Diversity, as a movement, attempts to legitimize and legalize most any cause, whether it be homosexuality, bisexuality, trans-genderism, polygamy, transracialism, or violent, mystical religions. Just because something is legal, does not make it right or proper.

What can pass for a religion? On a liberal arts college campus almost anything will be embraced. At the University of Southern

California the list of student religious organizations includes not only the well known religions of this world, but also Atheist, Falun Gong, Jain, Pagan, Wiccan, and Zoroastrian.[334]

SPECIFICS ON SPREADING ISLAMIC FASCISM TO COLLEGE STUDENTS

The book entitled <u>Unholy Alliance--Radical Islam and the American Left</u> reveals much about Islamic subterfuge in America. Moussa Abu Marzouk, leader of the Islamic terrorist group Hamas, launched a non-profit group called the "Holy Land Foundation." Their office was raided by the FBI in 2008 and shut down. Documents seized in the raid revealed that the Holy Land Foundation was part of a large network of organizations that Hamas had created earlier through Marzouk's efforts.

Included in that network was the Islamic Association for Palestine, the Council on American-Islamic Relations, al Qaeda, and more in particular, the Muslim Students Associations on universities throughout the USA. **A direct link to Muslim terrorists!** Many colleges are mentioned by name in the book. Muslim Student Associations on campuses are established and used to promote diversity through radical publications, lectures of faculty and demonstrations promoting Islam. Some of those colleges mentioned are Duke, Harvard, Columbia University, the University of South Carolina, Brown University, Northwestern University, the University of South Florida, Georgetown University, and UCLA.

---

334 http://orl.usc.edu/religiouslife/students/

There are Muslim Student Associations in many universities not mentioned in the book. Indiana University at Bloomington, Indiana, for example has an active, proselytizing Muslim Student Association in an otherwise conservative state. Gaining acceptance through the banner of diversity works in the minds of naive college students!

Here is one example of how Islam is promoted through college Muslim Student Associations. An engineering professor at South Florida University, Sami al-Arian, created a number of militant Islamic groups under the guise of free speech. While they were given harmless sounding names, such as: The Center for Constitutional Rights, World Islamic Studies Enterprise, and the Islamic Committee for Palestine, their underlying purpose was anything but harmless. Sami al-Arian visited mosques across America to raise funds, with a video advocating the killing of Christians and Jews, "and damning America until death." He was finally indicted as a terrorist, but it took seven years to do so because civil rights lawyers defended him as a victim.[335]

College students are prone, as are all young adults, to cling to a "cause." Because of the very liberal nature of college professors and universities in general in America today, college students are bombarded with bad ideas and seldom hear the other side of the story. It is no wonder that Islam is making inroads with America's youth. One author has catalogued and detailed the course material descriptions of over 200 college courses taught in American colleges today, which "actively indoctrinate students in leftwing ideology, not merely express a leftwing bias."[336]

---

335 <u>Unholy Alliance</u> by David Horowitz, 2004, 198-199
336 <u>The Black Book of the American Left</u> by D. Horowitz, 2013, p. 370

Militant Islam is daily going about its bloody aggression, making war against non-Muslims and Muslims alike to spread its control. At the same time, the subtle side of Islam is at work lulling America to sleep to the very real Fascist ideologies of Islam by presenting itself as a religion of peace!

America fought the political ideologies of Fascism in the form of Japanese emperor-worshipping Imperialists and German Nazis in World War Two. Once again, America is facing Fascism, only this time as Fascism disguised as religion, namely Islam. When something looks like a duck, walks like a duck and quacks like a duck, it is a duck.

The confrontation with radical Islam will only happen when Islam is recognized as a form of political Fascism, and dealt with as such. Islam is intent on world domination. Its containment and eradication of its destructive philosophy is essential to world peace. This means standing up against the various threats posed by Muslims, and taking broad, military action against the countries that spawn Islamic terrorism. After disarming Muslim terrorist groups and warring Muslim nations, then the free nations of this world would need to re-educate the citizens of these countries about human rights and freedoms. Those freedoms include the freedom of religion, as long as Muslims understand that waging war as part of Islam will not be tolerated.

The United Nations charter recognizes the right of every person to free speech and freedom of thought. Following World War Two, the Allies conducted public re-education programs in Germany and in Japan, to teach basic human rights including property rights, and democratically elected government, freedom of speech and freedom of religion. These were necessary elements of eradicating Fascism. Re-education will help stop the violence of Islamic peoples, who themselves are victims of the tyrannical political thought robed in a savage religion, in which they have been indoctrinated and enslaved.

Islam is conducting war continually against free people in the world as well as people living under Communism. War must be engaged against militant Islam as a whole, and not simply hunt for the perpetrators of the latest terrorist act. As enemy agents in World War Two infiltrated behind our lines, so likewise, Islamists have infiltrated our Armed Forces, as can be seen by the murder of 14 Army servicemen that were murdered by a U.S. Army officer who was a Muslim of Mid-eastern descent.

IT IS NO COINCIDENCE THAT FASCIST SYSTEMS ARE ALIKE--THREE LAST, DIRECT COMPARISONS

1. FASCISTS FORBID FREE THOUGHT: BOOK BURNING AND CENSORSHIP

Consider the subject of thought control, under Nazi Fascism and Islamic Fascism:

Nazi book burning and censorship

On May 10, 1933, something happened in Berlin, Germany, that had not happened since the Middle Ages. Hitler, in power less than six months, had ordered the works of dozens of German authors and many foreign authors destroyed. About 20,000 books were brought together and burned at the midnight hour opposite the University of Berlin.

Any thoughts and ideas that did not mesh with Hitler's Nazism were summarily banned. Measures were also formally instituted regarding the pre-approval from the Nazi government before any new book could be published. Nazi Propaganda Minister Joseph Goebbels addressed the crowd at the huge Berlin book burning that night:

> *"The soul of the German people can again express itself. These flames not only illuminate the final end of an old era; they also light up the new."*[337]

The authors of such banned and burned books were also hunted like animals in Germany and German-occupied countries by the Gestapo. The pursuit was well chronicled "...the Nazis were hunting down artists and intellectuals in France."[338] Escaping the German Gestapo net in Europe was a big challenge, especially since other nations of the world feared accepting or harboring intellectuals deemed radical by Hitler. With the 1940 armistice between Germany and France, intellectuals and artists were facing "extradition to Germany and certain death"[339] if captured.

---

337 The Rise and Fall of the Third Reich by William Shirer, 1960, p. 241

338 Villa Air-Bel by Rosemary Sullivan, 2006, p. 21

339 Ibid., p. 234

The book burning was a wake up call to some intellectuals in America. The journalist Eric Sevareid wrote:

"But we who had learned from history what the long struggle toward an age of reason implied knew the moment the Nazis burned the books that Fascism wanted war. We knew it in our bones."[340]

Who were some of the loathsome writers and authors whose works were burned and banned? Upton Sinclair, Andre Breton, Helen Keller, H.G. Wells, and Albert Einstein to name a few. Remember, Fascists claim the exclusive right to censor, to critique and to condemn what they will. To oppose this power, is to guarantee one's intimidation, punishment or death.

Islamic book burning and censorship

Islam's own version of thought control is an exact replica of the Nazis! Iran's revolutionary Muslim cleric Ayatollah Khomeini set the precedent, issuing his famous "fatwa" or legal opinion in 1989, that Salman Rushdie, the author of a fictional book entitled Satanic Verses and its publishers were condemned to die according to Islamic law. [341] According to Khomeini, Islam was insulted and blasphemed by Rushdie's book. This Muslim death decree in effect was an announcement that what Muslim authorities declare is the very force of law, anywhere on the planet. Such death threats have since become quite commonplace.

---

340 Not So Wild a Dream by Eric Sevareid, 1946, p. 64
341 Jihad: The Trail of Political Islam by Gilles Kepel, 2002, p. 186

Remember, Fascism involves intimidation. The idea is that threats against someone's life, which is a crime in itself in free countries, will help silence any opposition to the Fascist powers that be. What followed in this case was that Muslim residents of Bradford, England gathered for a public book burning of Rushdie's book on his home turf, Rushdie being a British citizen. Book burnings were also organized, accompanied by rioting and mob violence, in India and Pakistan against Rushdie's book. The book was subsequently banned in the majority of Muslim countries.[342]

When the book burning did not stop the further publication and distribution of Rushdie's book in England, a Muslim group sued in a British court to ban the book on the basis of religious discrimination. Happily for the institution of free speech and thought, the attorney general in Westminster, England, ruled that there were no grounds for British law to order the Satanic Verses book from circulation. Further street demonstrations against the book did not result in banning the book either.

The very real problem with censorship and death threats from Fascists is that Muslims actually believe that Muslim dogma is untouchable and immutable. In other words, any words spoken or written deemed offensive to Islam, are considered a crime against their god. Therefore Fascists believe they control all speech period. Naturally, free people are going to rebel against the fear and intimidation dealt by violent Muslim zealots. The alternative to rebelling against the threats behind Muslim censorship, is the eventual capitulation of free societies under Islamic

---

342 Ibid., p. 188

control of all speech, thought and expression as well as political, social and religious enterprises.

Free people usually are of the opinion that a good idea or doctrine should be able to stand on its own merit. If compliance toward some belief has to be forced on people by the threat of bombs and AK-47 assault rifles, then perhaps those beliefs ought to be questioned. But Fascists, being bullies, are not easily convinced by sound reasoning. This is sad news for the world because conflict ensues.

2. Fascists Enjoy Watching Executions

Nazi executions

There are many, many instances of photographing the bloody execution of Nazi prisoners. Some are too gruesome to describe. Here is but one example. In 1942, Czechoslovakia, being in the noose of Nazi occupation saw dozens, sometimes hundreds of Czechs murdered in the jails and prisons run by the Nazi Gestapo. These were civilians, many jailed without charges against them. The executions were by hanging, guillotine or firing squad:

> *"The neighbors spent a good part of their time on their knees, praying for the dying and the departed. The Gestapo agents, on the other hand, brought their wives and mistresses to watch the executions, which they did avidly, with enthusiasm and applause. For them it was wonderful entertainment."* [343]

---

343 <u>Tomorrow Will Be Better</u> by Zdena Kapral, 1990, p. 100

Islamic executions

Today, anyone with access to the internet can visit websites such as Al Jazeera, and watch videos of the beheading of kidnap victims of Islamic terrorists. This is taking place in various countries of the world where Islam is conducting armed violence. While this may be entertaining to some Muslims, it also serves the purpose of instilling fear of attack and kidnapping in the enemies of Islam.

3. FASCISTS TAKE HOSTAGES IN THEIR AGGRESSION

German hostage taking

As of the end of World War Two, Germany was the only country that had taken and used hostages in war. The first instance was in the Franco-Prussian War of 1870, when important French officials were made to ride in the engines of German trains to prevent enemy attack. In World War One, Germany made all the residents of villages walk along ahead of German soldiers advancing on the enemy, to stop enemy snipers from shooting. In World War Two, the German Nazis used hostages in battle in an attempt to protect themselves, as a matter of course.[344] This was cowardice.

Islamic hostage taking

Islamic terrorists routinely kidnap innocent civilians in places around the globe. Ransoms are sometimes arranged to recover victims if terrorists can arrange it. Unfortunately for the hostage(s), death by beheading usually follows sometime later. In 2015, this

---

344 <u>Underground Europe</u> by Curt Riess, 1942, pp. 238-239

kind of news could be heard on numerous occasions; the victims are aid workers, foreign diplomatic staff, journalists, and school children--virtually anyone that can be kidnapped. If the victims are female, they are kept as sex slaves or sold for money at the Islamic captor's sex slave market.

The Wake-Up Call has already sounded!
Today, Islam is the enemy! On May 28, 2014, U.S. Secretary of State John Kerry announced that the United States government was setting up a $5 billion "terrorism partnership fund" to assist other countries in pushing back against "radical extremists," according to the Associated Press. Note the politically correct wording, "radical extremists" rather than the truth of the matter, which would identify the problem for what it is--<u>Islamic</u> terrorism.

Just as the leaders of the free world understood in World War Two that Nazi Fascism had to be destroyed completely; we, too, must realize that there can be no compromising with Islamic Fascism today, it also must be destroyed completely. This was aptly expressed by General Dwight Eisenhower, Supreme Allied Commander of the Expeditionary Forces Europe expressed this truth about Nazi fascism:

> *"Daily as it progressed there grew within me the conviction that as never before in a war between many nations the forces that stood for human good and men's rights were this time confronted by a completely evil conspiracy with which no compromise could be tolerated. Because only by the utter destruction of the Axis*

was a decent world possible, the war became for me a crusade in the traditional sense of that often misused word."[345]

An apt description of Mohammedanism (now also called Islam or Muslim) was given by the man who shepherded England through World War Two, Prime Minister Winston Churchill. Mr. Churchill was a champion of the causes of free men. He wrote:

"How dreadful are the curses which Mohammedanism lays on its votaries! Besides the fanatical frenzy, which is as dangerous in a man as hydrophobia in a dog, there is this fearful fatalistic apathy. The effects are apparent in many countries. Improvident habits, slovenly systems of agriculture, sluggish methods of commerce, and insecurity of property exist wherever the followers of the Prophet rule or live. A degraded sensualism deprives this life of its grace and refinement; the next of its dignity and sanctity.

The fact that in Mohammedan law every woman must belong to some man as his absolute property – either as a child, a wife, or a concubine – must delay the final extinction of slavery until the faith of Islam has ceased to be a great power among men. Thousands become the brave and loyal soldiers of the faith: all know how to die but the influence of the religion paralyses the social development of those who follow it. No stronger retrograde force exists in the world. Far from being moribund, Mohammedanism is a militant and proselytizing faith."[346]

---

345 <u>Crusade in Europe</u> by Dwight D. Eisenhower, 1948, p. 157

346 http://www.dailymail.co.uk/news/article-2614834/Arrested-quoting-Winston-Churchill-European-election-candidate-accused-religious-racial-harassment-repeats-wartime-prime-ministers-words-Islam-campaign-speech.html

Current United States foreign policy sidesteps the issue of Islamic terrorism by focusing on the trees instead of the forest. A brief criticism of America's ineffectiveness in combating Islamic terrorism was given in an article by National Review Magazine online:

> *"After the laudable elimination of Osama bin Laden, there is currently no real war on Islamic terrorists, except for the NSA surveillance program, some remnants of the Bush–Cheney anti-terrorism protocols, and an under-the-radar drone targeted-assassination program, in which, acting as judge, jury, and executioner, the administration sends armed Predators to blow up suspected terrorists (and anyone unlucky enough to be near them) in Pakistan. Otherwise, both the world and the American public long ago ceased to care about workplace violence, man-caused disasters, overseas contingency operations, the promise of trials for terrorists in civilian courts, Miranda rights given to foiled bombers, renditions bad then good, Guantanamo rhetorically closed, the Muslim Brotherhood largely secular, and jihad little more than a personal journey. As of now, when innocent people are killed, as in the Benghazi attack, the president pontificates about tracking down the murderers — and the world tunes him out. Rogue nations — Iran, North Korea, Venezuela — now have little fear of the United States..."* [347]

---

[347] "America's New Anti-Strategy" by Victor Hanson, National Review magazine online, April 8, 2014 online at: (http://www.nationalreview.com/article/375215)

The liberal left in America: the enemy within

Former peaceniks in America now hold high government offices. U.S. Secretary of State, John Kerry, one would naturally expect to be the most ardent patriot because of the office which he holds. Because of the dangerous and radical accord Mr. Kerry has negotiated for the United States government with the country of Iran, his loyalties are brought into question.

The accord itself is very much akin to the agreements British Prime Minister Neville Chamberlain made with Adolf Hitler just prior to World War Two, which actually spawned war rather than prevented it because of the violent nature of paranoids, and because of the concessions granted to the enemy.

Secretary of State John Kerry, like many politically correct politicians who are willingly ignorant of the truth, made a statement about ISIS (also known as ISIL) in September, 2014. The statement, below, suggests that the extreme violence conducted by ISIS identifies the group as non-Muslim. This is to insinuate that Islam is a religion of peace. The truth of the matter is, that militant Muslims kill others, including Muslims, Christians and other non-Muslims regularly. Kerry said:

> *"Eliminating the ISIL threat...will mean demolishing the distortion of one of the world's great peaceful religions."*[348]

Since the date of that remark by Secretary of State Kerry, ISIS (referred to as ISIL by President Obama and friends) has butchered

---

348 <u>The Complete Infidel's Guide to ISIS</u> by Robert Spencer, 2015, p.27

thousands of Muslims and non-Muslims alike in Iraq and Syria, and continued their sex slave market, selling girls and women like cattle. ISIS is the true face of Koran-inspired Islam!

Consider John Kerry's recorded testimony in remarks from an earlier period of American history. His testimony made him anything but a candidate to represent the United States in matters of America's sovereignty and safety. As a U.S. Navy veteran of the Vietnam war, Kerry testified after his service there, about alleged atrocities commonly committed by U.S. armed forces in Vietnam.

His testimony was to the United States Senate Committee on Foreign Relations on April 23, 1971, on behalf of a group calling themselves the Vietnam Veterans Against The War. He associated himself with the anti-war left, and the likes of Jane Fonda and Tom Hayden who were pro-communist in their opinions of America's involvement in Vietnam. Included in Kerry's remarks before Congress were the following statements:

> *"We wish that a merciful God could wipe away our own memories of (our military) service...these were not isolated incidents but crimes committed on a day-to-day basis with the full awareness of officers at all levels of command."* [349]

The very idea of insinuating and indicting one's own American armed forces comrades in war with allegations of regular occurrences of criminal behavior against civilians in war, is very bold indeed.

---

349 <u>Unholy Alliance: Radical Islam & the American Left</u> by D. Horowitz, 2004, p. 237

And that such alleged crimes as mass murder by American soldiers and sailors would have been known and sustained without action to stop and punish such conduct by the entire chain of American military command, is ludicrous and irresponsible, if not treasonous!

President George Bush's response to the Islamic terror attacks on America on September 11, 2001 was to declare a global war on terror and the countries which allowed terrorists to domicile or train. It was a logical response to the cowardly murders of thousands of Americans on that infamous date.

United Nations inspectors had reported that there were sizeable quantities of biological chemicals for waging mass murder by chemical warfare unaccounted for, after inspections of Iraq's arsenals. Because of the danger to the people of Iraq and surrounding nations, with a resounding majority of Congress and the support of United Nations members (excluding Russia, China and France), the United States aided by Britain, invaded the country of Iraq in 2003 to dethrone its dictator, Saddam Hussein.

Unfortunately, though Saddam Hussein was taken from power and a provisional government established in Iraq, peace has not lasted in that country. In 2015, the Islamic terrorist group known as ISIS is at war to take over the country of Iraq (and other neighboring countries), battling against American-trained Iraqi armed forces and a coalition of other nations.

Though the Iraq war had the full support of the United States Congress, liberals in Congress have been quick to criticize the outcome. So much for spending $100 billion to deliver a country from a tyrant, at least in the estimation of one Congresswoman, Representative Nancy Pelosi.[350]

Liberal politicians in Washington went further still in their criticisms. After the Iraq war, liberals which had been supported our military action in Iraq, declared that the war never should have been conducted, and had been carried out in the worst possible manner by President Bush. This is the sort of partisanship and divisiveness which does not help America face the fact that Islam is the enemy, not our own leaders. The after-the-fact opposition to the war was, in general, only to advance the political hopes of people including John Kerry, Ted Kennedy and others.

Islam is a backward, savage Fascist ideology cloaked as a religion, and spread by violence and the threat of violence. Let us face the truth of the matter. Fascism seeks to kill the strong, seduce the weak and mislead the simple. America has seen many Islamic terrorist attacks resulting in mass murder: New York's Twin Towers on 9-11-2001, Fort Hood, Texas, the Boston Marathon bombing, the Marine Recruiting Centers in Chattanooga, Tennessee and others. But Islam is labeled as a minority religion, so it is off-limits because of political correctness, a euphemism to avoid facing obvious facts.

U.S. leaders are blind to ISIS (Islamic State)
President Barack Obama may well be a fervent, dedicated Muslim himself. Why? Because of the plainly incorrect appraisals of Mr.

---

350 <u>Unholy Alliance: Radical Islam & the American Left</u> by D. Horowitz, 2004, p. 223

Obama about the Islamic State of Iraq and Syria, or (ISIS) also known as the Islamic State (IS). Obama stated that "No religion condones the killing of innocents" and "The vast majority of ISIL victims have been Muslims."[351]

Obama said it. No religion condones killing innocent people. But we should know by now that Islam is not a religion by their campaign of terror. If, on the other hand, one considers Islam to be a religion, then Mr. Obama's statement is false because the plain truth is Muslims do kill other Muslims.

The fact that victims of ISIS include other Muslims, does not change the fact that the ISIS group has openly declared itself to be strict, Sunni Muslims that govern and rule by Sharia law.

Throughout the history of Islam, Sunni and Shia sects of the Muslim ideology have been marked by violent conflict, with much bloodshed. One historical example is a Sunni Muslim leader named Selim, who in the year 1514 A.D., gave the command to his followers to massacre 40,000 Shia Muslims. The hatred was so deep that Selim announced that the killing of one Shia Muslim would have a reward in the next life as if the follower had killed 70 Christians.[352]

Another more recent and well known instance of Muslim versus Muslim violence would be the eight year war between Iran and Iraq. Both were Islamic dictatorships, and were at war from 1980-1988. There were somewhere between 250,000-500,000

---

351 <u>The Complete Infidel's Guide to ISIS</u> by Robert Spencer, 2015, p.30
352 https://en.wikipedia.org/wiki/Shia_Islam

Iraqi Muslims and an estimated 1,000,000 Iranian Muslims who died in this war.[353] Muslims do kill other Muslims.

If ISIS is not Islamic, then it stands to reason that the major Islamic neighboring nations of Saudi Arabia, Iran, Pakistan, Egypt and/or others would be fighting against ISIS militarily in order to defend and preserve the lives and territory of fellow Muslim people and nations.

ISIS knows who they themselves are, and for what they stand. Consequently, ISIS has expressed their hatred and disregard of President Obama's denial that ISIS is Islamic. ISIS own internet publications have stated that President Obama is mistaken by his statements that ISIS is not Islamic, such as the ISIS declaration in September, 2014:

> "...And to the extent that Obama, the mule of the Jews, suddenly became a sheikh, mufti (Islamic scholar that issues verdicts) and an Islamic preacher, warning the people and preaching in defense of Islam, claiming that the Islamic State has nothing to do with Islam..."

The Obama Administration has put forth the fallacy that ISIS is not Islamic, despite the prolific pronouncements of ISIS itself, that they (the ISIS group) are **the** face of Islam. ISIS has openly stated its intent to bring all Muslim nations of the Mideast together under their Sunni Muslim rule for Islamic jihad.[354] The reason ISIS has shortened its name to the Islamic State (IS) is because they have de-

---

353 http://www.theguardian.com/world/2010/sep/23/iran-iraq-war-anniversarypass from memory into history.

354 The Complete Infidel's Guide to ISIS by Robert Spencer, 2015, p.274

clared themselves to be **THE** Islamic State and intend to do away with the other Muslim sovereign states, which they attest were divided up unnaturally by western nations that colonized Mideast areas into nation states.

Regarding ISIS, U.S. Secretary of State John Kerry parrots the President's fallacy about the group:

> *"The extremism that we see, the radical exploitation of religion which is translated into violence, has no basis in any of the real religions. There's nothing Islamic about what ISIL/ Daesh stands for, or is doing to people."*[355]

Kerry's statement is tantamount to calling Hitler's invasion of Poland a chamber of commerce welcome wagon. Is this misunderstanding by our leaders, of the continuation of Muslim violence under the current player ISIS simply ignorance, or is it willing ignorance?

Remember, Iran (Shia Muslims) created the Hezbollah terror group. Saudi Arabia (Sunni Muslims) gave the world Osama bin Laden's al-Qaeda terrorist group, and has provided funds to Hamas terrorists. Palestinian Muslims brought forth their terror group called Islamic Jihad to destroy Israel.[356] There are numerous other terrorist groups founded and funded by Muslim-run governments. Islamic terrorism has become a potent political force in the world ever since the Arab-Israeli war of 1973.[357] Their goal is the same as other Fascists have been: the takeover of the entire world.

---

355 Ibid., p.97
356 Jihad: The Trail of Political Islam by Gilles Kepel, 2002, p.123
357 Ibid., p. 5

ISIS (Sunni Muslims) has between 25,000 and 100,000 warriors fighting now in Iraq, Syria and elsewhere. ISIS now rules over more than 8 million people in a significant area of western Iraq and southern Syria. Significant numbers of these Muslim fighters have come from non-Muslim countries including Britain, France and the United States.

ISIS is causing mass migration of hundreds of thousands of Muslims, both Sunnis and Shias into western Europe. Is it out of fear of ISIS, or is it part of Muslim plans for takeover? No one knows, but ISIS is as violent or more so than any Muslim terrorist group has ever been. According to one well versed expert on the subject:

> *"ISIS constitutes a threat to the U.S. greater than that of al-Qaeda, Hamas, Hezbollah, Boko Haram and all other jihad groups combined."* [358]

If the Obama Administration and other western nations refuse to identify ISIS as a real and present danger to everyone, then the infiltration of Islamic jihadists will continue to accelerate into western Europe and America unabated. People are driven out of the Mideast by ISIS for fear of their lives, as the ISIS group operates as Sunni Muslims do, by the strictest Sharia laws governing every facet of life. Torture, murder, sexual enslavement and confiscation of property are all part of the ISIS program.

Why aren't the Sunni Muslim refugees welcomed into Sunni-controlled Saudi Arabia, the huge, neighboring oil rich country? It

---

358 The Complete Infidel's Guide to ISIS by Robert Spencer, 2015, p.xxii

is because ISIS is a different version of Sunni Islam than Saudis put forth. They therefore have not taken a single refugee fleeing ISIS in Iraq and Syria as of the end of 2015.[359]

And why aren't Shia Muslims headed east to seek refuge in Shia Muslim Iran? We may never know. One explanation, however, is that Islamist's goal is to have emigrants and their children ready and in place as future jihadists in western nations.

One professional Turkish smuggler admitted to guiding more than ten Muslim jihadists into western Europe through Turkey in 2014, at a cost of $2,500 per person. The smuggler would not specify just how many jihadists he had helped to emigrate, but did state that they were feigning themselves to be refugees.[360]

ISIS has boldly released details of its plans for the future. They include the conquering and takeover of Rome, Italy, by the year 2020. Rome is targeted because the headquarters of the Roman Catholic Church is located there, at Vatican City. Muslims remember the Catholic Crusades against them many centuries ago. Muslims also do not discern between Christian and Catholic, but instead refer to all Christians as "Cross worshippers."[361]

Another target named in published ISIS e-books is Israel, which ISIS declares will begin to see their end in the year 2022.[362]

---

359 http://sidroth.org/articles/saudis-refuse-syrian-refugees
360 The Complete Infidel's Guide to ISIS by Robert Spencer, 2015, p.63
361 Ibid., p.31
362 The Complete Infidel's Guide to ISIS by Robert Spencer, 2015, pp.266-273

The worldwide internet has made evil conduct much more widely available. ISIS, for example, has published on various websites, the details of how to construct bombs like the backpack bomb which was set off by Muslim terrorists at the Boston Marathon several years ago. ISIS published "Black Flags from Rome" in 2015, which details hit lists of journalists and cartoonists who are wanted dead or alive for insults to Islam, and ideas for Muslims to carry out "lone wolf" jihad attacks wherever a Muslim happens to live.[363] Such was the December, 2015 mass murder by Islamists in San Bernadino, California.

Islam is Fascism

What other "religion" on the planet could methodically slaughter 158 young Muslim boys in a school by gunfire, as Muslim terrorists did in Pakistan in December, 2014?[364] Why don't the news media outlets dwell on such unspeakable crimes against humanity? Will it take this sort of thing to happen to 158 children in a school in the United States for Americans to admit the peril and take steps to help eliminate the scourge of global Islamic Fascism? Unfortunately, it will probably take such a thing to happen before action is taken.

A central question to the eradication of all Islamic terrorism is whether America can unite against a common enemy. Islam has patently become that common enemy we must be willing to face

363 Ibid., pp.260-261

364 http://www.dailymail.co.uk/news/article-2875729/Up-20-dead-500-children-teachers-taken-hostage-Taliban-gunmen-storm-military-run-school-Pakistan.html#ixzz3kVPaRnti

and fight. General Dwight Eisenhower, Supreme Commander of Allied Forces in Europe in World War Two attested to America's willingness **then** to fight America's common enemy. He said:

> " *Victory in the Mediterranean and European campaigns gave the lie to all who preached, or in our time shall preach, that the democracies are decadent, afraid to fight, unable to match the productivity of regimented economies, unwilling to sacrifice in a common cause.*"[365]

How badly do Americans want to remain a free people? Do we wait to confront the violent nature of Islam until Islamic people represent a very potent minority in our government in Washington? We must not wait too long to face the very real problem of Islamic Fascism. Consider the lesson Prime Minister of England, Winston Churchill tried to convey about postponing or delaying necessary action against one's mortal enemy as England had done in its unpreparedness to meet Nazi aggression until the bombs began falling on English soil:

> *"Here was the righteous cause deliberately and with a refinement of inverted artistry committed to mortal battle after its assets and advantages had been so improvidently squandered. Still, if you will not fight for the right when you can easily win without bloodshed; if you will not fight when your victory will be sure and not too costly; you may come to the moment when you will have to fight with all the odds against you and only a precarious chance of survival. There may even be a worse case.*

---

365 <u>Crusade in Europe</u> by Dwight Eisenhower, 1948, p. 451

You may have to fight when there is no hope of victory, because it is better to perish than live as slaves."[366]

Religion and freedom can certainly co-exist. But if the religion is mixed with political control, as Islam is, then there is trouble. As one author expressed it:

"In authentic religions, God judges, God redeems and God forgives. In authentic religions, we understand ourselves as sinners. No one mistakes himself or herself as a redeemer. In political religions, on the contrary, human beings act as God, judging and condemning, and there will be no redemption. This is the bloody history of the left--the saga of the guillotine and the gulag, which continues now into the new millenium."[367]

America had better wake up to the fact that Islam is simply, old fashioned Fascism in a new wrapper. The goal of Islam is the destruction of so-called infidels, especially those that are Christians and Jews. America is called the Great Satan.

President Dwight Eisenhower gave a speech at the dedication of a new hydroelectric dam on October 19, 1953, in which he said of America and its neighbors:

"...Ours is the imperishable spirit of free men, unswayed by the cheap promises of totalitarianism, undismayed by its blustering threats..."[368]

366 The Gathering Storm by Winston Churchill, 1948, pp. 347-348
367 The Black Book of the American Left, Volume 5, Culture Wars, by David Horowitz, 2015, p. 320
368 Mandate for Change by Dwight D. Eisenhower, 1963, p. 240

Is the spirit of free men alive in America today? Our enterprises and our freedoms of speech and religion are an abhorrence to Muslims. But the wake-up call for America will come slowly because of corrupt liberal politicians, an anti-freedom of speech Supreme Court, and liberal, government-sanctioned news media.

How much more blood must be spilled before Fascist Islam is unmasked as a political ideology akin to Nazism, Communism and totalitarianism? If America is to remain a nation of free people, then Americans must face the problem of Islamic Fascism, or be overthrown by it.

Just as Germany employed so-called "fifth columnists" in every country where they intended an invasion and takeover, Muslims are emigrating to America for the same reason, in this author's estimation. Consider the hundreds of millions of dollars Arab countries are spending building Muslim mosques in the United States. Dearborn, Michigan, the home of Ford Motor Company, has had a literal invasion of Islamic people from the Mideast. Dearborn now has five Muslim mosques in that city and growing civil unrest precipitated by Muslims.

In 1938, an important German diplomat said "unless something intervenes, the policy of the Organization will help to bring us to war."[369] The Organization was the Fascist Nazi party. War is a natural by-product of Fascism. The goal of Islam today is hate-driven conflict and war, both civil war in America and war anywhere on the planet into which America can be drawn. Islamic jihad in its many forms is already well dispersed and underway. It

---

369 This Is The Enemy by Frederick Oechsner, 1942, p. 307

cannot be appeased, and must be confronted if America is to survive as a free country.

News correspondents in Europe at the close of World War Two witnessed the atrocities of Nazi Fascism first hand. They saw bodies of a hundred civilians massacred in a church yard. They witnessed other victims of Nazi executions who had been shot in the back of their heads. Shocked, they witnessed the horrors that had taken place in Nazi concentration camps. The same question the news men asked themselves back then about helping America awake to the terror of Nazi Fascism, could, and should be asked today of Islamic Fascism. That question was, is it better to make Americans angry about Fascism, or to frighten them about it?

Militant Islam must be destroyed, and the Muslims who would continue their Islamic faith must be taught that intolerance of and violence against other people will no longer be suffered by free nations. Freedom of religion guaranteed by the United States Constitution with its Bill of Rights does not include the right to commit violence against others who have different religious beliefs. The post-World War Two re-education of Japanese and German citizens about freedom of speech, freedom of thought, freedom of religion, and property ownership under freely elected leaders is a success story. It resulted in both nations being at peace with the rest of the world for over seventy years.

Most terrorists in our day are Muslims, and they are proud to identify themselves as Muslims.[370] When a terrorist carries out a

---

370 <u>The Crisis of Islam</u> by Bernard Lewis, 2003, p. 137

murderous attack, it is no surprise to anyone that the first name of one or more of the perpetrators is often Mohammed.

The task of changing violent and combative Muslim conduct of many of the 1.6 billion Muslims on the planet is a huge and difficult task. The masses who live under the violence associated with Islam under Sharia law, are accustomed to the savage behavior of Muslim rulers. It will be a slow process for those who have been under Muslim dictatorships to understand and respect the rights that freedom brings. This is because of the forced Islamic mentality that a person's life is not his own to live, and only the State matters.

After World War Two, German prisoners of war (POW) held in the United States were subjected to political and cultural lectures and films for their own good. Emphasis was on understanding such things as tolerance of others, and the benefit of competing political parties. The intent was not just about the positive aspects of freedom, but also covered the negative effects of Nazism which they had lived under. The learning in general came slow and with difficulty.

Documentary films shown to German POW's included films of Nazi death camps in Europe, including the emaciated survivors as well as actual stacks of dead human beings who perished there. Yet many German POW's who saw these films, refused to believe that Germany had actually carried out such mass murders. In fact, of 20,000 German prisoners surveyed afterwards, only 36% of them believed that what they saw had actually happened.[371]

---

371 <u>Prisoners of War</u> by Ronald Bailey, 1981, p. 169

Will America believe the peril that Islam poses? Germany attacked Russia suddenly in 1941 with an army of three million men, with the goal of annexing Russia into Germany. This happened just ten months after the two countries had signed a 10-year secretive, mutual non-aggression treaty!

Many advance warnings came to Russian leaders about the planned German attack on Russia. Those warnings were not taken seriously, because Russia trusted Germany's written intentions in the treaty guaranteeing peace between the two nations. Twenty million Russian civilians subsequently perished on Russian soil in the four year long war that followed, before the Nazi German aggressors were soundly driven out and defeated.[372] Actions do speak louder than words.

German Nazism and Russian Communism, two opposing evils, were nonetheless both Fascist in ideology and practice. Victor Serge, a famous Russian dissident, wrote about the Russian totalitarian State that it was "a concentration camp universe."[373] Stalin brooked no opposition to his rule of Russia, and used surveillance, mock trials, labor camps, starvation and outright executions to keep Russians in line.

We see this same form of aggression today between the different faces of Islamic Fascism, that of the Sunni and the Shia Muslim sects. The thing to remember is that whether it be the Fascists of World War Two or the Islamic Fascists of today, both are the enemies of free people everywhere.

---

372 <u>Russia Besieged</u> by Nicholas Bethell, 1979, pp. 26-31
373 <u>Villa Air-Bel</u> by Rosemary Sullivan, 2006, p. 62

America today is anything but secure. Our borders are open, and Congress does nothing to secure them. President Obama proposes to give illegal aliens a path to citizenship. He has also proposed to bring 70,000 or more Muslim immigrants to America from the troubled Mideast. Muslims are allowed in our armed forces, though Muslims around the world openly declare their intent to destroy America. Random acts of Muslim terrorism continue inside the United States.

There are more than thirty militant Islamic groups with headquarters in the United States right now. There are documented terrorist training camps on our soil, such as the training camp outside of Chicago, where Palestinian fighters have received training in the placement of car bombs.[374] There have been Muslim terrorist training camps for semi-automatic weapons discovered by State Police in Connecticut and another known to exist in New Jersey as well.[375]

Should America believe the talk that Islam is a religion of peace? Or should we not instead believe the acts of terrorism which are taking place in many parts of the world? Threats of destruction and death to America are made openly by Islamic dictators, clerics and terrorist groups. American high government officials and the news media would have Americans believe that Islam is a religion of peace! President Obama insists that Congress approve secretive treaties such as the treaty made with the Islamic Republic of Iran, a government which openly vows death to America in the cause of Islam. (And you don't think Obama is a Muslim?)

---

374 <u>American Jihad</u> by Steven Emerson, 2002, p. 81
375 Ibid., pp. 56-57

The point being, a nation cannot hope to <u>win</u> a war until it recognizes that there is a war going on. A nation cannot <u>fight</u> a war until it recognizes those who conduct war against it are its enemies. America cannot <u>defeat</u> Islamic terrorism until we first acknowledge that Islam is a Fascist, warring, political ideology.

Lisa Fittko, a Jewish journalist raised in Berlin, was one of the voices that warned the western world with news reports of Nazi Fascist tactics immediately after Adolf Hitler came to power in Germany in January, 1933. Fittko sent reports of torture chambers that had already been established in Germany, as well as details of the incarceration of intellectuals and dissidents in the first Nazi concentration camp at Oranienburg, Germany.[376] But the world did not heed her warnings or those of others who opposed Hitler's Nazi Fascism. Untold sufferings and death gripped the planet over the next twelve years because of Nazi Fascism, which took the lives of tens of millions of innocent men, women and children.

Islamic Fascism is at war against us now, intent on enslaving the freest nation on earth. How much blood will be shed before America admits the truth that Islamic actions speak much louder than words?

History offers us so many lessons. A description of the problem facing isolationist America as war spread across Europe in World War Two, was best described as a race:

"We were in a race; it was the rate of America's growing understanding versus the rate of the Fascists' physical advance."[377]

---

376 <u>Escape through the Pyranees</u> by Lisa Fittko, 1991, pp. 3-4
377 <u>Not So Wild a Dream</u> by Eric Sevareid, 1946, p.194

This is the essence of the problem with Islam today. Will America come to understand the evil nature of Islam before Muslims are in a position to permanently alter the American way of life, its constitutionally guaranteed freedoms notwithstanding?

In early March, 1945, near the close of World War Two, Winston Churchill made this statement:

"But we shall never, we shall never sit quietly by and permit a minority to force its will upon a helpless majority anywhere."[378]

However, in our present day, political correctness means evil intents of some minority interests including minority religions are allowed to fester and grow into significant problems for majority populations. Identifying Islam as a serious problem for any free western nation because of Islamic terror and human rights violations, is the first step in dealing with Islam before it becomes a much larger problem. Freedom and Islam are incompatible.

---

378 <u>A Soldier's Story</u> by Gen. Omar Bradley, 1999, p. 509

BIBLIOGRAPHY

A Soldier's Story by Gen. Omar Bradley, Modern Library Paperback Edition, Random House, Inc., New York, 1999

American College Dictionary by C.L. Barnhart, Editor, Random House, New York, 1963

American Dictionary of the English Language, by Noah Webster, First Edition, G & C Merriam Co., NY 1828

American Jihad: The Terrorists Living Among Us by Steven Emerson, Regnery Publishing, Inc., Washington, D. C., 2002

An Ordinary Camp by Micheline Maurel, Simon and Shuster, New York, 1958

An Uncertain Hour by Ted Morgan, William Morrow & Co., New York, 1990

Berlin Diary by William Schirer, Alfred Knopf Publishers, New York, 1941

Blood, Tears and Folly by Len Deighton, Harper Collins Inc., New York, 1993

Closing the Ring by Winston Churchill, Houghton Mifflin, Cambridge, MA, 1951

Coast Artillery Journal, Journal of the United States Army Artillery, Washington, D.C. May-June, 1946

Coast Artillery Journal, Journal of the United States Army Artillery, Washington, D.C. March-April, 1946

Colonial America by O.T. Bark, Jr. & Hugh Lefler, Macmillan Co., New York, 1968

Crusade in Europe by Dwight D. Eisenhower, Doubleday & Co., New York, 1948

Deadline by Pierre Lazareff, Random House, New York, 1942

Endgame: The Blueprint for Victory in the War on Terror by Lt. Gen. T. McInerny & Maj. Gen. Paul Vallely, Regnery Publ., Washington, D.C., 2004

Escape from Camp 14 by Blaine Harden, Penguin Group USA, New York, 2012

Escape through the Pyranees by Lisa Fittko, Northwestern University Press, Evanston, Illinois, 1991

Four Years of Nazi Torture by Ernst Winkler, Crowell-Collier Publishing Co., 1942

Foxnews.com/world news, June 28, 2015

From the Land of Silent People by Robert St. John, Halcyon House, Garden City, New York, 1943

German Psychological Warfare by Ladislas Fargo, G.P. Putnam's Sons, New York, 1942

Holy Bible, Authorized (King James), 1789, uncopyrighted

http://www.amnesty.org.uk/issues/north-korea

http://www.bbc.com/news/world-middle-east-14541327

http://www.childtrends.org/?indicators=births-to-unmarried-women

http://www.dailymail.co.uk/news/article-2614834/Arrested-quoting-Winston-Churchill-European-election-candidate-accused-religious-racial-harassment-repeats-wartime-prime-ministers-words-Islam-campaign-speech.html

http://www.dailymail.co.uk/news/article-2875729/Up-20-dead-500-children-teachers-taken-hostage-Taliban-gunmen-storm-military-run-school-Pakistan.html#ixzz3kVPaRnti

http://www.dailymail.co.uk/news/article-3186229/ISIS-executes-19-girls-refusing-sex-fighters-envoy-reveals-sex-slaves-peddled-like-barrels-petrol.html

http://elhambinai.blogspot.com/2007/09/prime-minister-of-australia-john-howard.html

http://www.infowars.com/what-does-isis-really-stand-for/David Stansfield

http://islamist-watch.org/blog/2015/07/reclaim-australia-demon-strations-and-counter

http://observer.com/2015/03/saudi-arabia-jordan-and-egypt-unify-to-battle-isis-is-iran-next/

http://orl.usc.edu/religiouslife/students/

http://www.religiousfreedomcoalition.org/2012/01/27/hate-crime-violence-by-muslims-on-upswing-in-michigan/

http://sidroth.org/articles/saudis-refuse-syrian-refugees

http:www.thehistoryplace.com, world war two in europe, timeline

http://travel.state.gov/content/passports/english/alertswarnings/

iran-travel-warning.html#

http://travel.state.gov/content/passports/english/alertswarnings/

worldwide-caution.html

http://www.wnd.com/2014/10/christians-bloodied-by-stone-throwing-muslims-in-michigan/

http://ww2.org/uk

http://worldnews.nbcnews.com/_news/2013/02/02/16788304-why-extreme-islamists-are-intent-on-destroying-cultural-artifacts?lite

https://www.cia.gov/library/publications/the-world-factbook/rankorder/2054rank.html

https://en.wikipedia.org/wiki/Algerian_Civil_War

https://en.wikipedia.org/wiki/Black_Stone

https://en.wikipedia.org/wiki/burqa

https://en.wikipedia.org/wiki/Berlin_Wall

https://en.wikipedia.org/wiki/Crusades

https://en.wikipedia.org/wiki/Iran#Religion

https://en.wikipedia.org/wiki/Malaysia

https://en.wikipedia.org/wiki/North_Korean_cult of personality

https://en.wikipedia.org/wiki/South_Korea

https://en.wikipedia.org/wiki/Taliban

https://en.wikipedia.org/wiki/Theo_van_Gogh_(film_director)

https://en.wikipedia.org/wiki/List_of_countries_by_unemployment_rate

I Paid Hitler by Fritz Thyssen, Wyman & Sons Ltd, London, 1941

I Will Bear Witness by Victor Klemperer, Random House, New York, 1999, p. 343

Is Germany Incurable? by Richard Brickner M.D., J. B. Lippincott Co., New York 1943

Israel Prime Minister Benjamin Netanyahu Speech to the United Nations General Assembly, September 24, 2010, New York, NY

Israel Prime Minister Benjamin Netanyahu Speech to U.S. Congress, March 3, 2015

Italy At War by Capt. Henry Adams, Time-Life Books, Inc., Morristown, NJ 1982

Japan at War, by Col. John Elting, Time-Life Books, Inc., Morristown, NJ 1980

Jihad: The Trail of Political Islam by Gilles Kepel, Harvard University Press, Cambridge, MA 2002

Journey Underground by David G. Prosser, E. P. Dutton & Co., NY, 1945

Korean War Almanac by Harry Summers Jr, Facts on File, Inc., New York, 1990

Last Train From Berlin by Howard K. Smith, Alfred Knopf Publishers, New York 1942

Liberators by Lou Potter, Harcourt Brace Jovanovich, New York 1992

Liberation by Martin Blumenson, Time-Life Books, Morristown, NJ, 1978

Mandate for Change by Dwight D. Eisenhower, Doubleday & Co., Inc., Garden City, NY, 1963

Master of Spies by General Frantisek Moravec, Doubleday, Garden City, NY, 1975

McGuffey's Fifth Eclectic Reader, Revised Edition, Fairfax Christian Bookstore, Tyler, TX, undated

McGuffey's Third Eclectic Reader, Revised Edition, Fairfax Christian Bookstore, Tyler, TX, undated

Men and Power by Henry J. Taylor, Dodd, Mead & Co., New York, 1946

Men in Motion by Henry J. Taylor, Doubleday, Doran & Co., Garden City, New York 1943

National Review Magazine online, article by Victor Hanson, April 8, 2014

Never Give In: Challenging Words of Winston Churchill by Price & Walley, Hallmark, 1967

Not So Wild a Dream by Eric Sevareid, Halliday Lithograph Corporation, West Hanover, MA, 1946

Our Battle by Hendrik Willem Van Loon, Simon & Schuster, New York, 1939

Paper Bullets by Leo Margolin, Froben Press, New York, 1946

Paris Underground by Etta Shiber, Charles Scribner's Sons, New York, 1943

Point of No Return by Wilbur Morrison, New York Times Book Co., New York, 1979

Prelude to War by Robert Elson, Time-Life Books, Morristown, NJ, 1977

Prisoners of War by Ronald Bailey, Time-Life Books, Morristown, NJ, 1981

Red Army Resurgent by John Shaw, Time-Life Books, Morristown, NJ, 1979

Russia Besieged by Nicholas Bethell, Time-Life Books, Morristown NJ, 1979

Sharia Law by Wikipedia, Wikimedia Foundation, 2014

Story of A Secret State by Jan Karski, Houghton Mifflin Co., Boston, 1944

The Aftermath: Asia by Col. John Elting, Time-Life Books, Morristown NJ, 1983

The Aftermath Europe by Douglas Botting, Time-Life Books, Morristown NJ 1983

The Anabaptist Story by William Estep, Broadman Press, Nashville TN, 1963

The Battle is the Payoff by Ralph Ingersoll, H. Wolff, New York, 1943

The Black Book of the American Left by David Horowitz, Encounter Book, New York, 2013

The Black Book of the American Left, Volume 5, Culture Wars, by David Horowitz, Second Thought Books, Sherman Oaks, CA, 2015

The Candy Bombers by Andrei Cherny, Penguin Group, USA, New York, 2008

The Complete Infidel's Guide to ISIS by Robert Spencer, Regnery Publishing, Washington, D.C., 2015

The Constitution of the United States Independence Hall, Philadelphia, 1787, reprinted by Heritage Foundation, Washington, D. C. 2010

The Crisis of Islam by Bernard Lewis, The Modern Library, New York, 2003

The Foe We Face by Pierre Huss, Doubleday, Doran & Co., Garden City, New York, 1942

The Gathering Storm by Winston Churchill, Houghton Mifflin Co., Cambridge, MA 1948

The Harvest of Sorrow by Robert Conquest, Oxford University Press, New York, 1986

The History of the Baptists, by Thomas Armitage, Maranatha Baptist Press, Watertown, WI, 1976

The Last Enemy by Richard Hillary, MacMillan & Co., Ltd., London, 1945

The Mind of the Founder, Sources of the Political Thought of James Madison, Brandeis University Press, Hanover, Waltham, MA, 1973

The Nazis by Robert E. Herzstein, Time-Life Books, Morristown, New Jersey, 1980

The Nazis Go Underground by Curt Riess, Doubleday, Doran & Co., Garden City, New York, 1944

The Candy Bombers by Andrei Cherny, G. Putnam & Sons, New York, 2008

The Past is Myself by Christabel Bielenberg, Chatto & Windus, London, 1972

The Political Writings of Thomas Jefferson by Merrill Peterson, Thomas Jefferson Memorial Foundation, Wolk Press, Woodland, MD, 1993

The Rise and Fall of the Third Reich, by William L.Shirer, Simon & Schuster, New York 1960

The Trail of Blood by J. M. Carroll, Southwestern Baptist Seminary, Ft. Worth, TX, 1928

The Well-Worn Fascist Lies of Putin editorial by Jonah Goldberg, Tribune Media, May 28, 2014

Their Finest Hour by Winston Churchill, Houghton Mifflin Co., Cambridge, MA, 1949

This Day in Baptist History by E. Wayne Thompson & David Cummins, Bob Jones University Press, 1993

This is the Enemy by Frederick Oechsner, Little, Brown & Co., Boston, 1942

This Is Where I Came In by Robert J. Casey, Bobbs-Merrill Co., New York, 1945

This Must Not Happen Again! The Black Book of Fascist Horror by Clark Kinnaird,, Pilot Press, 1945

<u>Time Runs Out</u> by Henry J. Taylor, Doubleday, Doran & Co., Garden City, NY, 1942

<u>Tomorrow Will Be Better</u> by Zdena Kapral, Harbinger House, New York, NY, 1990

<u>Top Secret</u> by Ralph Ingersoll, Harcourt, Brace & Co., NY, 1946

<u>Triumph and Tragedy</u> by Winston Churchill, Houghton Mifflin Co., Boston MA 1953

<u>Under Cover</u> by John Roy Carlson, American Book-Statford Press, Inc. New York, NY 1943

<u>Underground Europe</u> by Curt Riess, The Dial Press, New York, 1942

<u>Unholy Alliance</u> by David Horowitz, Regnery Publishing, Inc. Washington, D.C., 2004

<u>Villa Air-Bel</u> by Rosemary Sullivan, Harper Collins Publishers, New York, 2006

<u>Waging Peace</u> by Dwight D. Eisenhower, Doubleday & Co., Inc., Garden City, NY, 1965

www.ingramcontent.com/pod-product-compliance
Lightning Source LLC
Chambersburg PA
CBHW050436290526

45786CB00006B/2050